WATERS of EDEN

THE MYSTERY OF THE MIKVAH

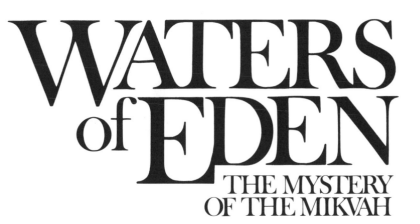

D1444457

ARYEH KAPLAN

Published by OU/NCSY Publications,
Orthodox Union, Eleven Broadway, New York, NY 10004.
212.563.4000 • www.ou.org.

Distributed by Mesorah Publications, Inc., 4401 Second Avenue,
Brooklyn, NY 11232. Distributed in Israel by Sifriati/A. Gitler
Books, 6 Hayarkon Street, Bnai Brak 51127. Distributed in Europe
by Lehmanns, Unit E, Viking Industrial Park, Rolling Mill Road,
Jarow, NE32 3DP, England. Distributed in Australia and New Zealand
by Golds World of Judaica, 3-13 William Street, Balaclava, Melbourne
3183, Victoria, Australia. Distributed in South Africa by Kollel Bookshop,
8A Norwood Hypermarket, Norwood 2196, Johannesburg, South Africa.

ISBN 1-879016-08-7

PRINTED IN THE UNITED STATES OF AMERICA

Susan Stein
8534 Shady Trail Cv
Cordova, TN 38018-4300

CONTENTS

A Publication

in the

JOSEPH TANENBAUM LIBRARY *Series*

There are things that stand in heights of the universe, yet people take them lightly.

Talmud, Berachos 6b.

INTRODUCTION

A friend of mine, who has visited Russia many times, tells of a secret meeting he had with a young Jewish family in a Russian city. After an involved discussion of the problems facing the community, my friend gained the confidence of the husband, a tall, sturdy man named Yaakov. As my friend was preparing to leave, Yaakov said, "Wait, I have something that I would like to show you."

He took my friend to the clothing closet. Before opening the door, almost instinctively, he looked over his shoulder, as if to make sure that no unwelcome eyes were watching. Satisfied that it was safe, Yaakov opened the closet, moved aside a number of boxes, and carefully lifted up a false floor. Under the floorboards there was a staircase, leading to a small pool. "This is the city's Mikvah," he proudly announced, "over forty families make use of it."

Yaakov then told my friend of the dangers involved in building that Mikvah. No religious facilities could be built without express government permission. Otherwise it was subject to the direst penalties. Besides, the house was government property, and if caught, he would face a long prison sentence for "defacing" it.

Gradually—almost cautiously—he began to tell how the Mikvah was built. All the work had to be done in the utmost secrecy. No one, even his closest friends and neighbors, could know what he was doing. Only a small amount of digging could be done under the house each day, so that the dirt could be disposed of without arousing suspicion. Small quantities of cement—"for making minor repairs"—were purchased, until there was enough to line the Mikvah. A similar subterfuge had to be used to obtain pipes for the plumbing. In addition, the rigorous requirements of Jewish Law had to be satisfied. This is difficult enough under any circumstances, even if secrecy is not a paramount consideration.

Not until the Mikvah was completed did Yaakov dare tell anyone about it. At first, his closest friends shared the secret. Gradually, one by one, other families were invited to make use of the hidden Mikvah. Most of them did not believe it possible—but they came anyway. Before long, Yaakov's "top secret project" had become the community Mikvah.

A year after this meeting, Yaakov and his family were finally able to emigrate to Israel. All of his children had remained observant Jews, even though they were born and raised in Russia.

When asked why he had undertaken all the expense and danger to build a Mikvah, Yaakov explained, "Without it, I could not live as a Jew."

One of the most exciting, recent archeological events in Israel was the excavation of the mountain fortress of Massadah. Here was the record of some of the last defenders of ancient Israel, who gave their lives eighteen hundred years ago for the holy soil.

Of all the fascinating discoveries on Massadah, one of the most important was the finding of not one, but two Mikvahs. Following the usual practice, one was most probably for men, while the other was for women.

Here were people fighting for their lives,—pitted against the might of the entire Roman Empire. Yet, on the mountain top of Massadah, they found the time and resources to build two Mikvahs. As religious Jews, they knew that they could not exist without them.

While the Massadah excavations were in progress, two experts on Mikvah, Rabbi David Muntzberg and Rabbi Eliezer Alter, examined them. After meticulous study, these rabbis announced that the Mikvahs had been built according to the minutest requirements of Jewish Law,—"among the finest of the finest, seven times seven." In the eighteen hundred years that have passed, neither the Mikvah nor its importance has changed.

In the past few years, the issue of conversion has received much publicity, especially in Israel. Even American news media have spoken of the term *Giur KeHalachah*—"conversion according to Jewish Law." Many people have begun to become aware of the fact that there are specific requirements involved in conversion to Judaism. One of these requirements is immersion in a Mikvah.

Conversion is an unique far reaching experience. It involves a change of identity, and the assumption of a new status, namely that of a Jew. It follows, therefore, that the rituals involved in conversion include those things that are most basic to Judaism.

The fact that the Mikvah is a necessary element in conversion indicates that it is an important element of Judaism. Indeed, anyone versed in Jewish tradition knows this to be true. The use of Mikvah is one of the main factors that traditionally distinguishes the Jew from the non-Jew.[1]

Many people would be surprised to learn that the Mikvah is more important than the synagogue. This may not be obvious, since in many communities, synagogues have expensive, imposing buildings, while the Mikvah is small and poorly maintained. Yet, the Mikvah is more important. Jewish Law maintains that a congregation that does not have its own Mikvah does not even have the status of a community.[2]

This is not mere theory. In Israel, where religious authorities are particularly meticulous, the Mikvah is the first religious facility that is built in a new community. It is of primary importance. Synagogue services can be held in an apartment or store. The synagogue building is erected later, when the community is better organized and established.

Typical structure of a modern Mikvah

VISITING A MIKVAH

Many people have never seen a Mikvah, and even if you have seen a Mikvah, you might have missed many details. Therefore, at this point, it may be useful to paint an imaginary picture of a typical Mikvah.

At first glance, a Mikvah looks like little more than a small swimming pool. The water is usually about chest high, large enough for three or four people to stand in comfortably. For easy access, there are stairs leading into the water of the Mikvah.

If you look more closely, you will see a small hole, two or three inches in diameter, just below the water line of one wall of the pool. This hole may appear insignificant, but it is what actually gives this pool its status as a Mikvah.

Just opposite this small hole, you will notice a removable cover over a *Bor* or "pit," which is the essential part of the Mikvah. This *Bor* is a small pool by itself, and it is filled with natural rain water. The rain water must enter the *Bor* in essentially a natural manner, as will be discussed in a later section. Under certain conditions, spring water or melted snow or ice can also be used.

There are two other requirements for the *Bor* aside from containing natural rain water. First, it must contain at least forty *Sa'ah*. The *Sa'ah* is an ancient Biblical measurement, equivalent to approximately five gallons of water, so that the Mikvah contains approximately 200 gallons of rain water.

The second requirement is that the *Bor* must be a pit built directly into the ground. It cannot consist of any kind of vessel that can be disconnected and carried away, such as a barrel, vat or tub. Under some conditions, however, it can be built directly into the upper story of a building.

The *Bor* itself can be used for a Mikvah, but since it is very difficult to change its water, it is most often used as a source to give another pool connected to it the status of a Mikvah. This larger pool can be filled in any convenient manner from the ordinary city water supply, and its water can be changed as often as desirable. The only requirement is that it be connected to the water of the *Bor* by an opening at least two inches in diameter. By connecting the two pools and allowing their waters to mingle we give the water in the larger pool the status of the water in the smaller pool. The process of intermingling the waters of the two pools is known as *Hashakah*, this too will be discussed in more detail in a later section.

Now that we have some idea of what a Mikvah looks like, we can briefly mention its uses. There are three basic areas where immersion in the Mikvah is required by Jewish Law:

1. After a woman has her monthly period, she may not be intimate with her husband until she immerses in the Mikvah. This involves a Biblical law of the utmost severity.

2. Immersion in a Mikvah is an integral part of conversion to Judaism. Without immersion, conversion is not valid. This is required of men and women alike.

3. Pots, dishes and other eating utensils manufactured by a non-Jew must also be "converted" by immersion in a Mikvah before they can be used on a Jewish table. This is a special law in its own right, and does not necessarily have anything to do with Kashrus.

Besides these, there are other times when it is customary to use the Mikvah. For example, it is an established custom to immerse before Yom Kippur as a sign of purity and repentence. Many Chasidim immerse before the Sabbath in order to sensitize themselves to the holiness of the day. In this general context, immersion in a Mikvah is a process of spiritual purification and cleansing.

In ancient times, the Mikvah had another important function in relation to various types of *Tumah*, or ritual defilement.

WHY MIKVAH?

If we look at the commandments found in the Torah, we find that they fall into three major categories. Firstly, there are what we would call moral and ethical laws, the need for which is fairly obvious. Thus, when the Torah tells us not to steal, kill, cheat or hurt another's feelings, we do not have to look far to understand the reasons for such rules. These are moral laws, and are necessary if men are to live together in harmony. These commandments are known as *Mishpatim,*—translated literally, "judgements." Any person with good *judgement* should find this category of laws and commandments perfectly obvious.

Secondly, there are other commandments, which, while not morally necessary, fill an important need in strengthening Judaism. These are the rituals and festivals which reawaken us to important religious truths or commemorate key events in Jewish history. For example, few people would question the importance of observing Passover, which commemorates the Exodus from Egypt. Indeed, it is one of the best kept of Jewish holidays. The same is true of the Sabbath and other holidays. Similarly, commandments such as Tefillin and the Mezuzah serve constantly to remind us of God's presence. Commandments in this second category are known as *Edos*—literally, "witnesses." These are the practices that bear *witness* to the important concepts of Judaism.

7

The third category, is the most difficult to understand. It consists of laws and commandments for which there is no apparent reason. The best known example are the dietary laws, for which no explicit reason is given, either in the Torah or in Talmudic literature. These commandments serve to strengthen the bond between God and man, but the manner in which they do this is by no means obvious. Laws falling into this category of commandments are known as *Chukim*, translated literally as "decrees." These are commandments which we must obey as *decrees* of our God, whether or not we understand their reason.[3]

One of the most important commandments falling into this last category is that of Mikvah.[4]

It is obvious that this category of commandments is the most difficult to keep. The Talmud tells us that these are the laws that "the Evil Urge (*Yetzer HaRa*) and the nations of the world attempt to refute."[5] If we do not understand the reason for something, it is tempting to find excuses not to do it. When we try to explain our religion to non-Jews, the laws that do not have an obvious reason are the most difficult to justify. If a person is unsure of himself or is wavering in his Judaism, these laws will be the first to be abandoned. This may well explain why the use of the Mikvah has become one of the most neglected observances, and even—God forgive us—a joke in some circles.

The fact that a commandment does not have an obvious reason makes its observance all the more an act of faith. It indicates that we are ready and willing to obey God's commandments, even when we cannot justify them with logic. It shows that we are placing God above our own intellect.

In this spirit the Jewish people accepted the commandments. The Torah relates that when Israel accepted the Torah, their initial response was (*Exodus 24:7*), "All that God says, we will do and we will hear, (*Na'aseh VeNishma*)." Our sages stress the fact that their first statement was "we will do," and only then did they say, "we will hear." This indicates that when the Torah was given, we were ready to keep the commandments and "do" them, before we "heard" any reason or logic for them.[6]

The Talmud illustrates this with an anecdote. A gentile saw the sage Rava engrossed in his studies. So involved was he that, although he had crushed his finger, causing it to bleed profusely, he was oblivious of the pain. The gentile remarked, "You are an impetuous people, allowing your mouth to precede your ears—and you are still not aware of what you are doing. At first you should have heard all the reasons, and then you could have decided whether or not to accept the Torah."

Rava replied, "We went into it with complete trust. Is it not written (Proverbs 11:3), "The integrity of the upright shall guide them?"[7]

When we keep commandments that have no apparent reason, we demonstrate our inner security as Jews. Even though we may not be able to justify these commandments to the world, we feel secure as Jews to continue observing them. We understand what the Torah means when it says, (Deuteronomy 4:6), "Observe and keep [the commandments], for this is your wisdom and understanding in the eyes of the nations." We do not observe the commandments because logic demands it, but simply because they were given by God. The required basis is the relationship between the commandments and their Giver. This is higher than any possible human wisdom.[8]

This may be one reason why a convert to Judaism must immerse in the Mikvah. The convert's first step into Judaism involves a ritual whose explanation is not apparent and obvious, and therefore, he must reaffirm the initial acceptance of the Torah, declaring, "I will do and I will hear." To abandon his gentile identity and to assume Jewish identity, he is required to participate in a ritual that is inexplicable to one who does not accept the basis of Judaism. By so doing, he demonstrates his status as one who keeps those commandments "that the Evil Urge and nations of the world try to refute."

The fact that we are required to observe certain commandments without awareness of their reason does not mean that there is no logic in their observance. The reasons involve deep concepts that are not immediately obvious. When we realize that there is a limit beyond which we cannot delve, we can begin to explain their significance.

In ancient times, one of the main uses of the Mikvah was for ritual purification. There were numerous things that would render a person *Tomeh* (ritually unclean). The main significance of such *Tumah* was that a person in that state was forbidden to enter the grounds of the Holy Temple in Jerusalem (*Bais HaMikdash*). Violation was punishable by the severest penalties.[9] The Torah speaks of numerous things that make a person *Tomeh*, ritually unclean, and of a number of processes of purification. One act of purification that is required in all cases, is immersion in the Mikvah.[10]

The laws of ritual purity and impurity belong in the category of commandments known as *Chukim*, decrees for which no reasons are given. These laws were to be taken on faith, because they were given by God, as indicated by the teaching of our sages who said, "The dead body does not defile, and the water does not cleanse. Rather, God said, 'I have issued an order, and made a decree—and no man may violate My decree.' "[11]

From these words we see that the Mikvah involves some degree of spiritual purification. In a later section, we will define "pure" (*Tahor*) and "impure" (*Tomeh*) more carefully, and thus gain a greater insight into these concepts.

Up until this point, we have stressed the fact that there is no explicit reason given for the Mikvah and its associated laws. Nevertheless, we can strive to understand the significance of these laws.[12] However, we must realize that the reasons which will be discussed provide only an incomplete picture, and that the ultimate rationale of such commandments is beyond the grasp of human intellect. Therefore, no matter how deeply we probe, these reasons cannot serve to change or restrict these religious laws.[13] No matter how profound these reasons may be, we must realize that the Torah emanates from God, and that His commandments may involve many factors beyond the grasp of our mind and experience. With this in mind, we can begin to probe the reasoning underlying the Mikvah.

On the simplest level, we usually think of water as a cleansing agent. If one is bodily unclean, it is natural to wash with water. Therefore, when we think of purification and cleansing in the spiritual sense, we would also use water as the purifying agent. It is the special status of the Mikvah that allows us to cleanse ourselves spiritually, as well as bodily.[14]

If we look into the Torah more carefully, we find that the Mikvah has a deeper significance than mere purification, particularly in two special areas.

The first involved the original consecration of Aaron and his sons as *Kohanim* or priests, which took place soon after the exodus from Egypt, and was administered by Moses. Aaron and his sons then served as priests in the *Mishkan* sanctuary built in the desert, and their descendants have retained this special status for all time. Even today, a *Kohen* is an individual whose lineage goes back directly to Aaron in an unbroken line.

The Torah tells us that the first step in the consecration of Aaron and his sons as *Kohanim* involved immersion in a Mikvah.[15]

Here, immersion did not involve "purification," but rather, a change in status—an elevation from one state to another. Aaron and his sons were originally no different than anyone else, but with this immersion they attained the new status of *Kohanim* or priests.

The second area where we see the special significance of Mikvah is in the Yom Kippur service in the Holy Temple (*Bais HaMikdash*). This service is outlined in the sixteenth chapter of Leviticus. Although this special Temple ritual has not been performed for over 1900 years, its detailed retelling provides some of the most dramatic elements of our current Yom Kippur *Mussaf* service.

The most crucial part of this ancient Temple service was the entrance of the High Priest (*Kohen Gadol*) into the Holy of Holies—the special chamber in the Temple where the ark containing the original stone Tablets given to Moses was kept. This was the only time of the year when any human being was allowed to enter the Holy of Holies. The *Kohen Gadol* had to put on special white vestments before entering this most sacred room. After leaving the Holy of Holies, he would once again put on the "golden" vestments that he wore all year round.

On this most sacred of days, the *Kohen Gadol* would enter the Holy of Holies two times. This, in turn, would require that he change his vestments five times, since he would begin and end in his "golden" ones. Each time before he changed, he would have to immerse himself in a Mikvah.[16]

The *Kohen Gadol* was not impure or unclean in any way. He was rather undergoing a change in status, symbolized most dramatically by the changes of vestments. When he entered the Holy of Holies, he had a very different status than before—a unique status that would allow him to enter this room. This change in status was achieved through immersion in the Mikvah.

The immersion in ritual purification involves the very same concept. The water is not washing away any filth. Rather, the Mikvah is changing the individual's spiritual status from that of *Tomeh* (unclean) to that of *Tahor* (clean). Actually, this "purification" is a change of status rather than a "cleansing" process.

The most dramatic example of this change of status is in the case of conversion. Here again, there is no question of uncleanness or purification, but merely a change in status.[17] As in the examples mentioned earlier, this change in status comes about through immersion in the Mikvah. As the Talmud states, "as soon as [the convert] immerses and emerges, he is like a Jew in every way."[18]

How does immersion in a Mikvah change a person? This can best be understood on the basis of another Talmudic teaching, that "a convert who embraces Judaism is like a new born child."[19]

This has many important ramifications, especially with regard to the convert's (previous) non-Jewish family. In addition, it provides us with an important insight into the concept of Mikvah, that emerging from the Mikvah is very much like a process of rebirth.

Seen in this light, we see that the Mikvah represents the womb.[20] When an individual enters the Mikvah, he is re-entering the womb, and when he emerges, he is as if born anew. Thus he attains a completely new status.

This is particularly true in the purification from ritual uncleanness. The womb is a place that is completely divorced from all concepts of *Tumah* and uncleanness. A baby enters the world in complete purity, and there is no way in which he can be defiled while in the womb.[21] Thus when an individual enters the Mikvah, he leaves all uncleanness and *Tumah* behind, and emerges as a new, purified person.

The indentification of the Mikvah with the womb becomes somewhat clearer in view of the fact that the Torah describes the world's most primitive state as water. In the opening verses of the Torah, we find (*Genesis 1:2*), "The earth was empty and desolate, with darkness on the face of the deep, and God's spirit fluttering *on the face of the water.*" On the second day of creation, the "upper waters" were divided from the "lower waters." Finally, on the third day, the waters were gathered into seas, so that dry land could appear.

In a sense, therefore, water represents the womb of creation. When a person immerses in the Mikvah, he is placing himself in the state of the world yet unborn, subjecting himself totally to God's creative power.[22]

We can see this from the etymology of the world *Mayim*, which is the Hebrew word for water. According to a number of authorities, it shares the same root as the word *Mah*, meaning "what."[23] When a person immerses in water, he is nullifying his ego and asking, "What am I?" Ego is the essence of permanence, while water is the essence of impermanence. When a person is ready to replace his ego with a question, then he is also ready to be reborn with its answer. Thus, when Moses and Aaron declared (*Exodus 16:7*), "We are *what*," our sages comment that this was the greatest possible expression of self nullification and subjugation to God.[24] When a person enters the Mikvah, he subjugates his ego to God in a similar manner.[25]

We can also see this in a more prosaic manner. When a person immerses himself in water, he places himself in an environment where he cannot live. Were he to remain submerged for more than a few moments, he would die from lack of air. He is thus literally placing himself in a state of non-existence and non-life. Breath is the very essence of life, and, according to the Torah, a person who stops breathing is no longer considered among the living.[26] Thus, when a person submerges himself in a Mikvah, he momentarily enters the realm of the nonliving, so that when he emerges, he is like one reborn.[27]

To some degree, this explains why a Mikvah cannot be made in a vessel or tub, but must be built directly in the ground, for in a sense, the Mikvah also represents the grave. When a person immerses, he is temporarily in a state of nonliving, and when he emerges, he is resurrected with a new status.[28]

The representation of the Mikvah as both womb and grave is not a contradiction. Both are places of non-breathing, and are end points of the cycle of life. Indeed, it is interesting to note that the Hebrew word *Kever*, which usually means a "grave," is also occasionally used for the womb.[29] Both are nodes in the cycle of birth and death, and when a person passes through one of these nodes, he attains a totally new status.

In one place, our sages liken a person who immerses in the Mikvah to seeds planted in the ground.[30] Even though such seeds may be *Tameh*, ritually unclean, the plants that grow from them have a new status, and are clean.[31] The seeds have been returned to their source, where they can once again begin the cycle of growth. When the new seedlings emerge from the ground, they retain no element of their previous ritually unclean state. The same is true of man. For him, the waters of the Mikvah are his womb and source, and when he emerges, he too is like a new individual.

We therefore see that immersion in the Mikvah represents renewal and rebirth. We will examine this concept in greater detail, but first, let us take a closer look at just what a Mikvah is.

WHEN THE MIKVAH IS USED

NIDDAH

The most general use of Mikvah is for the purification of a woman after her monthly period. Although this primarily involves married women, it has important ramifications for single girls as well.

According to the Torah's definition, a woman has the status of a "Niddah" from the time that she has her period until she immerses in a Mikvah. The Torah thus states (*Leviticus 15:19*), "When a woman has a dicharge of blood, where blood flows from her body, she shall be a Niddah for seven days." As we shall see, she retains this status until she immerses in the Mikvah.

The word Niddah comes from the word *Nadad,* meaning "removed" or "separated."[1] The very word therefore indicates that she must forgo all physical contact with her husband. The word Niddah does not refer to menstruation, but to this necessity for separation. Both the name and the status of a Niddah are retained by a woman until she changes this status by immersion in a Mikvah.

The Torah openly forbids any sexual contact between a man and any woman who has the status of a Niddah. We thus find the commandment (*Leviticus 18:19*), "You shall not (even) come close to uncovering the nakedness of a woman who is 'unclean' as a Niddah."[2]

Sexual intercourse between a man and a woman with the status of Niddah is considered a most serious sin. The Torah tell us (*Leviticus 20:18*), "If a man lies with a woman who is a Niddah, and uncovers her nakedness, . . . both of them shall be cut off from their people."

The expression, "they shall be cut off," refers to the penalty of *Korais.* This is the same penalty that we find for incest between brother and sister,[3] violating Yom Kippur, or eating bread on Passover.[4]

The expression "cut off" does not refer to any type of mutilation or excommunication. Rather, this is a spiritual penalty, where a person is "cut off" from his spiritual source.[5] The individual loses the ability to feel and appreciate the spiritual and Godly, and thus becomes "cut off" from the most important elements of life as a Jew. The only way for a person to re-attach himself to his spiritual source is to sincerely repent before God with resolve never to repeat the act.[6]

The prohibition against sexual contact between a man and a woman who is a Niddah is a most serious one. This is perhaps best expressed in the words of the Prophet Ezekiel, who says (Ezekiel 18:5, 6), "If a man is righteous, and would accomplish justice and charity. . . . He will not defile his neighbor's wife, nor will he approach a woman who is a Niddah." The prophet equates intercourse with such a woman to adultery with another man's wife.

The fact that a woman removes herself from the status of Niddah by immersion in a Mikvah is known primarily from the Oral Torah, which was transmitted by God to the Jewish people at Sinai, along with the written Torah.

Like many other things in the Oral Law, this too is alluded to in the written Torah. The Torah says regarding a Niddah (Leviticus 15:28), "She shall count seven days, and then she shall be purified." After counting seven "clean days," a woman must undergo a normal process of ritual purification. As we have seen, the universal means of such purification is immersion in a Mikvah, and this is also required to remove the status of Niddah.[7] Even though the prohibition against sex for a Niddah is not directly related to ritual impurity (Tumah), the means of changing this status is likened to a purification process.[8]

Another allusion to the fact that the status of Niddah is removed by water is found in the Torah's discussion of the immersion of vessels. The Torah states (Numbers 31:23), "It shall be pure only if it is purged in water for a Niddah." According to the Talmud, this indicates that vessels must be immersed in a Mikvah, just like a Niddah.[9]

The fact that a Niddah had to immerse, was well established in the Oral Torah, even without these allusions. We see that the Prophet takes it for granted when he says (Zechariah 13:1), "On that day, a fountain shall be opened, for the house of David, and for the inhabitants of Jerusalem, for purging and for the Niddah."[10] From this, we clearly see that it was a well established fact that a Niddah required immersion for her purification.

Use of the Mikvah is one of the most important aspects of Jewish married life. In a sense, it is even more important for the marriage bond than the wedding ceremony and can be seen as a monthly renewal of the couple's marriage.

Like most of the laws involving Mikvah, those involving Mikvah are "decrees" or *Chukim*, for which the Torah gives no reason. Nevertheless, like all these laws, it has an innate underlying logic.

The Talmud, provides one "reason" that is related to our discussion. Since the rules of Niddah require a woman to be physically separated from her husband at least twelve days each month, the couple experiences a virtual honeymoon after the wife's immersion. Unlike many couples, whose sex life becomes almost dull and jaded after a number of years, a husband and wife keeping the rules of Niddah experience continual renewal. [11]

Many couples who begin to keep these strictures late in marriage report a new zest in their relationship. During pregnancy, when the Niddah cycle in interrupted, many couples eagerly anticipate a return to the separation periods and the monthly "honeymoon" that the Niddah laws provide.

The rules involving Niddah and Mikvah are fairly involved, and every engaged or married couple should attempt to familiarize themselves with them. Classes are held in many larger communities, and any competent rabbi would be happy to provide literature and other information for interested couples. In general, however, the main requirement is that a woman count seven "clean" days in the ritually prescribed manner after her period ends, and then remove her Niddah status through immersion in a Mikvah.

Although the laws of Niddah are usually discussed within the context of marriage, they are equally important to single girls. From the time a girl begins to menstruate, she assumes the status of Niddah, whether she is married or not. [12] From the time of her first period, until she immerses in the Mikvah with marriage, she retains this status.

This has many important ramifications. Judaism forbids

premarital intercourse in the strictest terms. Even if a girl has not yet begun menstruating, or in the rare case where she has immersed since her last period, premarital intercourse is still forbidden. The Torah states (*Deuteronomy 23:18*), "There shall be no harlot among the daughters of Israel." According to the Torah's definition, harlotry includes all forms of premarital sex, and has nothing to do with payment for the act. Thus, any couple engaged in premarital intercourse is violating the commandment forbidding harlotry.

CONVERSION

Another important use of the Mikvah involves conversion. As we discussed earlier, immersion in the Mikvah is an integral part of the conversion process, without which a non-Jew cannot enter the ranks of Judaism. In the case of a male, immersion must be preceded by ritual circumcision, while for a woman, immersion itself represents the entire ritual of conversion.

When a convert embraces Judaism, he is actually repeating what the Jewish people did when they first came into existence.

The special relationship between God and Israel was established for all generations through an oath and a covenant. The Torah spells this out when it says, (*Deuteronomy 29:9-14*):

> *You are all standing before the Lord your God . . . to enter into the covenant of the Lord your God—and into His oath—which the Lord your God is making with you today—that He may establish you this day as His own people, and that He may be your God, as He promised you, and as He swore to your fathers, Abraham, Isaac and Jacob. It is not with you alone that I am making this covenant and oath . . . but also with those who are not here this day.*

These verses mention two things with which the Torah was accepted, an oath and a covenant.

The oath was taken shortly after Israel crossed the Jordan and entered the Promised Land under Joshua. The entire nation of Israel stood between Mount Ebal and Mount Gerizim, and the oath was administered by the Levites. The oath, prescribed by the Torah, provides that the Levites should declare (*Deuteronomy 27:26*), "Cursed is he who does not uphold the words of this Torah and keep them—and all the people shall say Amen."[15] With this, all generations of Jews became bound to keep the Torah as if each one had personally made an oath to abide by it.[16]

The covenant was made before the giving of the Ten Commandments at Sinai. It consisted basically of three things, circumcision, immersion in the Mikvah, and a sacrifice.[17]

The circumcision of all males took place before the first Passover, just prior to the Exodus from Egypt. The Torah states that the Passover could not be celebrated by one who was uncircumcised, and therefore all the males who celebrated the first Passover had to be circumcised. We thus find that (*Joshua 5:5*), "all the people who came out [of Egypt] were circumcised."[18]

The second part of the covenant was a sacrifice, that was brought on behalf of the entire Jewish nation just before the giving of the Torah. We thus find (*Exodus 24:5-8*), "And [Moses] sent young men of the children of Israel, who offered burnt offerings . . . to God. . . . And [the people] said, 'All that God has spoken, we will do and we will hear (*Na'aseh VeNishma*).' . . . And [Moses] said, 'This is the blood of the covenant that God has made with you.' "

The final part of the covenant consisted of all the people immersing in the Mikvah. Immediately before the Ten Commandments were given, we find that God told Moses (*Exodus 19:10*), "Go to the people, and sanctify them today and tomorrow, and let them *wash their garments*. And be ready for the third day, for on the third day, God will descend in the sight of all the people on Mount Sinai."

The command to "wash their garments" seems puzzling, until we look into the general laws regarding purification. There, we find that whenever a person is required to "wash his clothing," he is also required to immerse himself in the Mikvah. When the Torah states that an individual must wash his clothing, this means that he must purify his clothing *as well as* his body in the Mikvah. Thus, we know from tradition that an important part of the preparation for the receiving of the Ten Commandments consisted of immersion in the Mikvah.[19]

We find another allusion to this in a most beautiful parable given by the Prophet Ezekiel. He likens Israel to an abandoned child, who was cast aside by her parents at birth. God takes in this infant girl, caring for her and raising her to be a princess. God then says (*Ezekiel 16:8, 9*), "Your time was the time of love. I spread My garment over you, and covered your nakedness. I swore to you, and I entered into a covenant with you—says the Lord God—and you became Mine. Then I washed you in the water. . . ." This washing refers to the immersion of the Jews before the giving of the Ten Commandments. [20]

When a person converts to Judaism, he must enter the covenant in the same manner as Israel did when they first accepted the Torah. The Torah thus says (*Numbers 15:15*), "As you are, so shall the convert (*Ger*) be before God."[21] Every male who converts to Judaism must therefore undergo the special ceremony of ritual circumcision. If he is already circumcised, "blood of the covenant" (*Dam Bris*) must be drawn. Both men and women must then undergo immersion. When the Holy Temple (*Bais HaMikdash*) stood in Jerusalem, and the sacrifical system was in force, the third element of conversion involved bringing a sacrifice. This sacrifice, however, is not required now that the Temple is no longer standing and the sacrificial system no longer exists.

The ritual of immersion, as well as circumcision where required of a male, is not something a convert can do on his own. Since it involves a major change in a person's communal status it must be treated as a community function. Therefore, these rituals are administered by a three man rabbinical court. Unless done in the presence of such a court, conversion is not valid. [22]

Immersion in a Mikvah is not only the main ritual of conversion, but was also the means through which all Jews originally entered into the covenant with God. Mikvah has its roots at Sinai as one of the earliest Jewish rituals.

There is even evidence that the ritual of immersion goes back to the time of the Patriarchs. One of the main differences between Abraham and other religious people who lived before him is that Abraham was deeply concerned with others, and taught those around him concerning God. Not only did Abraham spread God's teachings, he began the new faith that was to become Judaism. According to tradition, Abraham literally converted people to this new faith. [23] This tradition of converting others was followed by Isaac and Jacob. [24]

The question then arises, how did Abraham convert those who wished to enter his new faith? We find a hint in the story of the three angels who visited Abraham. Abraham's first remark to them was (*Genesis 18:4*), "Let now a little water be taken, and wash your feet." The Zohar explains that this alluded to the fact that Abraham had a Mikvah, and immersed the strangers in it.[25] The reason feet were specified for washing was because he suspected that they might be idolators, who "bow down to the dust of their feet."[26] According to this, the ritual of immersion in a Mikvah originated with Abraham.

POTS AND DISHES

The last area where the use of a Mikvah is required by Jewish Law is for pots, dishes, and other eating utensils. Of all the uses of Mikvah, this is perhaps the least known, but is nevertheless of major importance.

Briefly, the law requires that any metal or glass eating utensil manufactured or owned by a non-Jew, be immersed in a Mikvah before it can be used for Jewish food.[27]

This rule has nothing to do with Kashruth. Rather, this immersion is a form of "conversion" for the utensils, very much like that required for a person who converts to Judaism.[28] Thus, it is even required for brand new utensils, that have never been used before. When a utensil has been used for non-Kosher food, it must be both "Kashered" (rendered Kosher), and immersed.[29] The rules for Kashering are too complex to be included here, and a competent rabbinical authority should be consulted where this is required.

Before the immersion of metal or glass utensils previously owned by a non-Jew, the following blessing is said:[30]

בָּרוּךְ אַתָּה יְיָ אֱלֹהֵינוּ כֶּלֶךְ הָעוֹלָם אֲשֶׁר קִדְּשָׁנוּ בְּמִצְוֹתָיו וְצִוָּנוּ עַל טְבִילַת כְּלִי (לרבים כֵּלִים):

Baruch Atah Ad-noy El-henu Melech HaOlam Asher Kid'shaNu BeMitzvoSav VeTzivaNu Al Tevilas Keli (Kelim).

Blessed are You O Lord, our God, King of the universe, Who made us holy with His commandments and commanded that we immerse a utensil (utensils).

This is similar to the blessing *Al HaTevilah* (upon immersion) said by both a Niddah and a convert when they immerse in the Mikvah.

The law requiring that utensils be immersed is derived primarily from the Oral Torah.[31] Nevertheless, it is alluded to in the written Torah in a most interesting context.

Toward the end of the Jews' forty years in the desert after leaving Egypt, shortly before they crossed into the Promised Land, they came near the land of Moab. The Torah tells us

24

that (*Numbers 25:1, 2*), "the people began to commit harlotry with the daughters of Moab. And [the Moabite girls] called the people to sacrifice to their gods, and the people ate and bowed down to their gods." As a result, war eventually broke out between the Israelites and the Moabites. The Israelites emerged victorious and brought back a considerable amount of spoil.

God then commanded them (*Numbers 31:22, 23*), "The gold, the silver, the copper, the iron, the tin, and the lead—everything that comes through fire, you shall bring through fire—and it shall be pure only if it is purged in water for a Niddah. And everything that does not come through fire, you [need only] bring through water."

The Torah tells us that the metal utensils the Israelites brought back as spoil had to undergo a special purification before they could be used. If they were cooking utensils that were used over fire—which "comes through fire"—they would have to be Kashered (made Kosher) by heating in fire, as is indeed the law.[32] This, however, is not enough. Before these vessels could be used, they would also have to be "purged in water for a Niddah"—that is, immersed in the same kind of Mikvah required for a Niddah.[33] Utensils not used over fire need only be washed thoroughly and immersed.

From this we learn two things. First, we see that all metal utensils made by a non-Jew must be immersed before they can be used. Secondly, we learn that when vessels must be Kashered, this should be done before their immersion.

Our sages liken the table to an altar, and therefore, every utensil used on a Jewish table must be sanctified, just like vessels used on the altar of the Holy Temple (*Bais HaMikdash*).[34] This is part of a Jew's sanctifying every element of his life.

Like all the other laws involving Mikvah, this one is a *Chok* or "decree," for which no reason is given. Indeed, in introducing this rule, the Torah openly states (*Numbers 31:21*), "This is the decree (*Chukah*) of the Torah, which God commanded Moses." Nevertheless, this rule still has a degree of logic.

The use of metals represents one of man's major steps toward civilization. Rabbi Samson Raphael Hirsch explains that a metal utensil is therefore the most visible sign of man's intelligent mastery over the earth and its materials.[35] Not only the shape, but the use of the material itself proclaims this fact.

This explains why metal vessels have a special status. Since glass is processed and melted like metal, it also has this status.

Eating, on the other hand, is an activity that primarily belongs to the animal sphere of man's nature. When a metal utensil is used for eating, this therefore represents man's highest mental faculties being employed to serve his animal nature.

The Torah requires, however, that even the most physical of man's activites be elevated to the realm of the spiritual. Before using a metal utensil for eating, we must first sanctify and elevate it to a level of holiness by immersion in a Mikvah.

The vessel will, in turn, sanctify the food served in it. In this manner, a Jew's eating utensils become like the consecrated vessels of the Holy Temple, which sanctified anything that was placed in them.[36]

CUSTOMS

In the cases discussed earlier, Niddah, conversion and utensils, immersion in the Mikvah is required by Torah law. There are a number of other cases where immersion in a Mikvah is customary. In such cases, no blessing is said upon immersion.

It is customary for a repentent apostate to immerse in a Mikvah. A person who "converts" to another religion is still considered a Jew, and does not require any formal conversion when returning to Judaism. Nevertheless, it is customary for him to immerse, as a sign of repentence and spiritual rebirth.[37]

Immersion in the Mikvah is an act of self-renewal and rebirth, and therefore, it is customary to immerse as a sign of repentence. For this reason many religious Jews immerse before Yom Kippur, and indeed, this custom is brought in the codes.[38] Some also immerse before Rosh HaShanah.[39]

Since immersion in the Mikvah indicates a change in status, many people, particularly Chassidic Jews, follow the custom of immersing on Friday afternoon as part of their preparation for the Sabbath. The Sabbath is on a completely different spiritual level than the other days of the week, and immersion in the Mikvah indicates this change of status.[40]

It is customary to immerse three times when going to the Mikvah. One reason for this is because the word Mikvah occurs three times in the Torah.[41]

A DEEPER LOOK

THE RIVER FROM EDEN

> *God planted a garden in Eden,
> to the east, and there He placed
> the man that He had formed. And
> God made the ground grow every
> tree that is pleasant to see and
> good to eat—and the Tree of Life
> in the middle of the garden, and
> the Tree of Knowledge of Good
> and Evil. And a river went out of
> Eden to water the garden, and
> from there it split, and became
> four headwaters. . . . And God
> took the man, and placed him in
> the Garden of Eden to work it and
> to watch it. And God commanded
> the man, saying, "From every
> tree of the Garden, you may eat.
> But from the Tree of Knowledge in
> the middle of the Garden, you
> may not eat—for on the day you
> eat from it, you will die.*
>
> Genesis 2:8-17

This account tells of how God created man, and then placed him in the Garden of Eden, which represents the perfected state of man. Man was given one commandment, to abstain trom eating the fruit of the Tree of Knowledge. As the account ends, the serpent tempts Eve and both she and her husband eat the forbidden fruit. Man is then driven from the idyllic life of the Garden of Eden, and must live in the world outside. This represents the imperfect state of man today.

However, there is one puzzling element in this account. Right in the middle of the story, the Torah suddenly speaks of the river that came out of Eden, giving a detailed descrip-

30

tion of the river and its tributaries, interrupting the narrative for no apparent reason. This is all the more puzzling, since the river is never again mentioned in the entire account. Furthermore, the entire story of Eden teaches us a very important lesson about man and his condition, and in this context, the description of the river seems all the more out of place.

In order to explain the inclusion of the rivers, we first must grasp the concept of man's perfection, the concept of evil, and the idea of Adam's sin.

Every basic question that we can ask about Judaism begins with one fundamental question: Why did God create the world? Of course, to a large degree, this question is unanswerable. We cannot understand God, and we certainly cannot understand His reasons. Still, we can probe those reasons that God Himself revealed in His Torah and to His prophets.

What we learn from these sources is that God created the world as an act of pure altruism, in order to do good.[1] He created a world, and placed man upon it, in order that man be the recipient of this good.

What is this good that God desired to give man? Our sages teach us that God's intention would not be satisfied with giving anything less than the ultimate good.

But, what is the greatest possible good God can give to man? The answer is that the greatest possible good is God Himself. Therefore, the good that God destined for man was the ability to resemble Him and draw close to Him.[2]

In order for this to be possible, man had to be created with absolute free will. Otherwise, he would be little more than a puppet or a robot. With free will, on the other hand, man is created "in the image of God."[3] "Just as God acts as a free Being, so does man. Just as He acts without prior restraint, so does man. Just as God can do good as a matter of His own free will, so can man.

Just as man must have free will, so must he have freedom of choice. A man locked up in a prison has the same free will as anyone else, but still, there is little he can do with it. For man to resemble his Creator to the greatest degree possible, he must function in an arena where he has the maximum freedom of choice. The more man resembles God in His omnipotence, the closer he resembles Him in His free choice of good.

In order to make this freedom of choice real, God had to create the possibility of evil.[4] If nothing but good were possible, there would be no freedom of choice, and the good would produce no beneficial change. To use the Talmudic metaphor, it would be like carrying a lamp in broad daylight.[5]

Originally, however, this evil was not an integral part of man. Man was a perfectly integrated creature, who had no inner desire or compulsion to do evil. To the contrary, man's natural inclination was to live in perfect harmony, both with his environment and with his spiritual self. As such, man had no conflicts, frustrations, compulsions or lack of self control. He had the ability to build a perfect society, where each individual could grow, develop, and serve God to the best of his ability.

This was the state of man in the Garden of Eden. He lived an idyllic life, with no work or toil, with his mind free to contemplate wisdom, and his soul free to commune with God.[6] His food was right at hand, and he had need for neither clothing nor shelter.[7]

Evil was not part of man, but an outside force he could easily avoid. This was represented by the Serpent in the Garden, which was not part of man's makeup, but something outside of him. Man could debate with this evil or ignore it, like any other outside force. Evil urges and compulsions were not part of him, as they are now, so that now he cannot escape them, no matter where he goes.[8]

Man was given one commandment, not to eat of the Tree of Knowledge of Good and Evil. In this Tree, good and evil were intermingled, in such a manner that they could not be separated. Once man partook of this tree, the same became true of him.

At that moment, evil became an intrinsic part of his being. He now had a *Yetzer HaRa*,—an Evil Urge—that was part of his psyche, and no matter what he would do, he could not escape it.[9] Just like the Tree of Knowledge, man was now a mixture of good and evil, and he would have to spend all his days fighting this evil and attempting to overcome it.

Man's very essence now became filled with contradictions. His life became full of conflict and its resulting frustrations, making a perfect society all but impossible. Man's spiritual nature and animal nature became two opposites, in constant conflict, causing mental anguish and imperfection.

In man's perfected state, represented by the Garden of Eden, he would have been able to attain physical as well as spiritual perfection. Ultimately, he would have vanquished death and gained immortality. When man sinned and ate from the Tree, he lost this opportunity to gain immortality. God therefore said regarding the Tree of Knowledge (*Genesis 2:17*), "On the day that you eat of it, you will surely die."[10]

Since the entire world was created for the sake of man, when man fell, he brought the entire world down with him. Evil would no longer be concentrated in a single "serpent," but would now be diffused throughout all creation. Just like in the Tree of Knowledge, good and evil would be completely intermingled, and man would have to struggle to discern one from the other.

God eventually chose the Jewish people to recreate the state of Eden, and thus eventually elevate all mankind. To enable them to accomplish this, He gave Israel the Torah. For one thing, this gave man the ability to overcome the evil in himself,[11] it also gave him the ability to avoid evil, overcome it, and eventually elevate it to a state of good.[12]

This is a very important point. In his fallen state, man cannot attain good by himself, nor can he reach out to God on his own. The only way to attain good, approach God, or form a perfect society, is through the Torah. As a result of Adam's sin, evil has become such an integral part of man, reinforced by hundreds of generations of sin, that the only means for man to escape it and overcome it is through the specific remedy given by God, and that remedy is the Torah. Our sages therefore teach us that God said, "I have created the Evil Urge, but I have created the Torah as its remedy."[13]

One of the important commandments that God gave Israel was to build a Sanctuary (*Mikdash*). He thus told us (*Exodus 25:8*), "They shall make Me a sanctuary (*Mikdash*) that I may dwell among them." When Israel was in the desert, this Sanctuary took the form of the prefabricated Tabernacle (*Mishkan*) that was carried with them on their journeys. When they finally settled in the Promised Land, it was built as the Holy Temple (*Bais HaMikdash*) in Jerusalem.

But the question arises, why was it necessary to have a special sanctuary? We know that, (*Isaiah 6:3*), "the whole earth is filled with His glory."

Our sages teach us that the reason for the Sanctuary was because the entire world had become intermingled with evil as a result of Adam's sin. When God chose Israel, He told them to build one Sanctuary where this evil would not enter. This Sanctuary was to be like a miniature Garden of Eden, devoted totally to the service of God, where everything pertaining to man's fallen state would be excluded.[14]

This explains the concept of *Tumah*, or ritual uncleanness. The main application of the rules regarding such ritual uncleanness was with regard to the Sanctuary or Holy Temple (*Bais HaMikdash*).[15] Normally, it made no difference whether a person was ritually clean or unclean. When he was in an unclean state, however, he was absolutely forbidden to enter the Holy Temple, under the severest of penalties. The Torah thus says (*Numbers 19:20*), "But the man who is unclean, and does not purify himself, that soul shall be cut off from the community if he defiles God's Sanctuary."[16]

But what is this concept of uncleanness? Obviously, such uncleanness is not physical. Rather it is a type of spiritual defilement that places a person in a state in which he is forbidden to enter the Holy Temple. We learn that it is spiritual when the Torah says (*Leviticus 11:44*), "You shall not make your *souls* unclean. Thus, ritual uncleanness is something that primarily involves the soul, rather than the body.[17]

Ritual uncleanness is often associated with sin. We find in God's words to His prophet (*Ezekiel 14:11*), "They shall no longer make themselves unclean through their sins." Uncleanness is ultimately related to evil and sin.[18]

Things that cause ritual defilement are primarily associated with death. Thus, many kinds of ritual defilement are caused by contact with dead bodies or dead animals.[19] Other causes of uncleanness are things that are associated with man's imperfection.

Ultimately, all uncleanness is a result of Adam's sin.[20] Death and all other human imperfection was a result of this sin. If man would have remained in his elevated state in the Garden of Eden, nothing would exist that could cause uncleanness.

This explains why a person who has been defiled by something unclean was not allowed to enter the grounds of the Holy Temple. The Temple represents a miniature Garden of Eden. When Adam sinned, he was driven from this Garden. Therefore, anything associated with this sin prevents him from entering the miniature Garden of Eden that is the Temple. When a man is in a state of *Tumah* or uncleanness, he may not enter the Temple grounds under the severest of penalties.[21]

But how does man purify himself and remove himself from this state of uncleanness? How does he disassociate himself from man's fallen state and reassociate himself with Eden?

This purification is primarily through water, through immersion in the Mikvah. Water is the primary connection that we have with the Garden of Eden.

The Talmud tells us that all the water in the world ultimately has its root in the river that emerged from Eden.[22] In a sense, this river is the spiritual source of all water. Even though a person cannot re-enter the Garden of Eden itself, whenever he associates himself with these rivers—or with any other water,—he is re-establishing his link with Eden.

We thus find a Midrash which tells us that after Adam was driven from Eden, he repented by sitting in this river.[23] Although he had been permanently barred from the Garden itself, he tried to maintain a link through this river.

Thus, when a person immerses in the waters of the Mikvah, he is also re-establishing a link with man's perfected state. He then loses the status of uncleanness (*Tumah*), and is reborn into a state of purity, where he is permitted to enter the Holy Temple.[24]

This also explains why the Mikvah must be linked to natural water. Water must come to the Mikvah from its natural state, and must not come in contact with man in his state of spiritual exile. Similarly, it must not pass through anything that is capable of becoming defiled, since this would also break its direct link with the River from Eden.

Our sages thus teach us that the word MiKVaH (מִקְוֶה) has the same letters as Ko(V)MaH (קוֹמָה), the Hebrew word for "rising" or "standing tall." [25] It is through the Mikvah that man can *rise* from things associated with his fallen state, and re-establish a link with the perfected state that is Eden.

We can now go back to our original question. The story of Eden is interrupted with a description of the "River that ran out of the Garden of Eden." In the beginning of this section, we questioned the significance of this river. By now, the reason for the river is apparent. The Torah tells us that God planted a Garden, and in it, the Tree of Knowledge of Good and Evil. With it, the possibility was created that man would sin, and be evicted from Eden. Thus, even before God placed man in Eden, He established a link between the Garden and the world outside, namely the river which emerged from Eden.

The account of this river is therefore not an extraneous fact that merely interrupts the story. Rather, it is an important statement regarding man's condition in the world outside of Eden. Even though man has been expelled from Eden, a link remains. The concept of Mikvah is very closely associated with this link.

THE ELECTION OF ISRAEL

One of the most difficult questions regarding Judaism involves the concept of the "chosen people." If God created the world to bestow good on man, why did He not give all mankind access to this good? Why was the Torah, which is the main gateway to this good, only given to Israel? In short, why did there have to be a single "chosen people?"

The answer to these questions brings us back to Adam. When man was first created, all mankind was destined to be the "chosen people." If Adam had not sinned, then all of his children would have been worthy of partaking in the ultimate good that God destined for all mankind.[26]

When Adam sinned, however, the opportunity was lost for all his children to automatically be included in this concept. As a result of the evil that had become part of man's nature, the early generations forgot God almost completely. Only a few individuals kept alive the tradition of serving the one true God.

Our sages teach us that "there were ten generations from Adam to Noah. . . . All these generations continued to anger [God], until He finally brought the flood upon them."[27]

God gave mankind these ten generations to lift themselves back up to the state of Eden. If they would have done so, all mankind would again have had a chance to become the Chosen People. The Midrash thus teaches us that God intended to give the Torah to the generations of Noah.[28] That generation, however, was so evil, that it could not accept the Torah. Instead of having the waters re-establish their link with Eden, the generation of Noah was destroyed by them. If water could not rectify man by purifying him, it would do so by destroying all who were unworthy.

Soon after the flood, however, the world again reverted to paganism and corruption. With very few exceptions, man again forgot the rule of God. Again, there were ten generations,—this time from Noah to Abraham.

Although born into a pagan atmosphere, Abraham spent his life seeking and serving God. He realized that he could not live a truth while allowing others to be ignorant of it, he therefore became the first to publicly teach others about God and His law. Unlike other righteous men, Abraham was able to establish his faith among his descendants, until a self-sustaining group was formed. The Torah tells us that God said of Abraham (*Genesis 18:18, 19*), "Abraham shall surely become a great and mighty nation, and all the nations of the earth shall be blessed by him. For I have known him, and I know that he will instruct his children and household after him, that they may keep God's way. They will observe righteousness and justice, in order that God may bring upon Abraham everything that He promised him."[29]

During Abraham's lifetime, the Tower of Babel was built and mankind was divided into many nations. This took place when Abraham was 48 years old.

In Abraham, God saw a force that could bring all mankind back to Him, and regain the status of the "chosen people." God therefore brought a spirit of unity into the world, influencing all mankind to act with one accord. Under the leadership of Abraham, they could all have been restored to the state of Eden. Instead, mankind united to build the Tower of Babel.[30]

Man then lost the opportunity for all humanity to become the "chosen people." Instead, mankind was divided into nations. The Torah thus says that (*Genesis 11:9*), "[God] confounded the language of all the [people of the] earth, and . . . scattered them abroad upon the face of the earth."

Each nation was then given its own language and mission. God decreed that the children of Abraham would also become a nation, with the special mission of serving God.[31] Regarding this, the Torah says (*Deuteronomy 32:8, 9*),

> *When the Most High gave the nations inheritance, when*
> *He separated the sons of man,*
> *He set the borders of the peoples according to the number*
> *of Israel's children;*
> *For God's portion is His people, Jacob, the lot of His*
> *inheritance.*[32]

The other nations, were given one last chance to gain the status of the "chosen people." The Midrash tells us that, before giving the Torah to Israel, God "offered" the Torah to all the other nations, who, in turn, "refused" to accept it.[33] God looked deeply into the essence of all these nations, and saw that none of them would be able to preserve the Torah for thousands of years and not abandon it. Thus, Israel alone was worthy to receive the Torah and become the chosen people.

The Torah is the means through which the Jew elevates himself back to the state of Eden. Therefore, the Jews had to immerse in a Mikvah before receiving the Torah.[34] Through the waters of the Mikvah, the link with Eden was re-established.

The same holds true for any person who converts to Judaism today. He must also re-establish this link with Eden, since this is a fundamental element of the concept of the chosen people. This is one reason why a convert to Judaism must immerse in the Mikvah.[35]

The final state, where all mankind will partake of God's good, is in the World to Come. At that time, all the world will once again be in the state of Eden. The prophet thus foretold (Isaiah 51:3), "[God] will make its desert like Eden, and its wastelands like the Garden of God." When this time arrives, the entire world will be clean, and uncleanness will cease to exist. God thus said (Zechariah 13:2), "I will cause . . . the spirit of uncleanness to be removed from the earth."

This will be a time when all mankind will attain the perfection that was originally destined for it. All the world will once again be in a state of harmony and perfection, and the strife and conflict that afflicts mankind will cease to exist. God thus told His prophet (Isaiah 11:9), "They shall not hurt nor destroy on all My holy mountain, for the earth shall be full of the knowledge of God, just like the waters cover the sea."[36]

Here again we find the concept of water. The knowledge of God is likened to "the waters that cover the sea." In the Future World, it will be as if the waters of Eden have covered all the world. Mikvah alludes to the "waters of knowledge," that will ultimately encompass all mankind.

THE HOLINESS OF SEX

Among the most difficult commandments to understand are those associated with Niddah and menstruation. The Torah tells us that from the time a woman has her period, until she immerses in the Mikvah, she has the status of a Niddah. During this period, all sexual activity and physical contact with the opposite sex is forbidden.

Like all other such laws, Niddah is a *Chukah* or "decree," for which no reason is given. Still, it does have a logical basis, which we will attempt to explore.

A common source of confusion is the fact that a taboo against a menstruating woman is found in many primitive societies. Many such societies place harsh restrictions on a woman during her monthly period. This has led some misguided writers to declare that the Torah laws regarding Niddah are merely an extension of these primitive beliefs and practices. In order to properly appreciate the significance of the Torah laws, we must contrast the reasons for them with the reasons for these primitive taboos.

First, however, we must understand the nature of menstruation. From the time a woman reaches puberty, she loses a relatively small quantity of blood at the end of her menstrual cycle each month. This blood loss, which is called the menstrual flow, is intimately related to the human reproductive process. Every month, a woman releases an ovum or egg, which, if fertilized, becomes an embryo which will grow into a new human being. The lining of the uterus (endometrium) thickens to accommodate the fertilized egg. It develops an increased blood supply with which to nourish the embryo if the egg is fertilized.

If the egg is not fertilized, after approximately two weeks, it is expelled. The uteral lining and its accumulated blood is also shed, and the expelled material is essentially what constitutes the menstrual flow. Thus, the menstrual cycle involves the construction and destruction of an enriched uteral lining.

This well-known fact is by no means that simple or logical. From a biological standpoint, it would be much more economical if the uteral lining would be reabsorbed instead of expelled. This would certainly be more esthetic and comfortable for the woman. She would then not have to lose a significant amount of her vital fluids each month.

Even more efficient, from a biological viewpoint, would be a situation that would allow the womb to remain in a constant state of readiness to nourish the fertilized ovum. Actually, there is no biological or medical reason why the uteral lining must be expelled and restored each month. There is no reason why the ovum has to "die" only to be replaced by another egg. Most biologists look upon this as an example of unexplained inefficiency in the human reproductive system.

To the primitive mind, which had no idea of the inner workings of the womb, the very idea that a woman should lose a portion of her vital fluids was both bizarre and frightening. They could not explain it logically, and therefore, they attributed it to some "evil force." According to most anthropologists, this is one of the main reasons so many taboos surround the menstruating woman in many primitive cultures.

We see, however, that all of our biological sophistication does not really help us understand this natural phenomenon. With all our scientific knowledge, it still remains an "unexplained inefficiency of the human reproductive system." In *The Second Sex*, Simone de Beauvoir writes of menstruation:[37]

> *This complex process, still mysterious in many of its details, involves the whole female organism, since there are hormonal reactions between the ovaries and other endocrine organs, such as the pituitary, the thyroid, and the adrenals, which affect the central nervous system, the sympathetic nervous system, and in consequence, all the viscera. . . . The woman is more emotional, more nervous, more irritable than usual. . . . It is during her periods that she feels her body most bainfully as an obscure, alien thing; it is, indeed, the prey of stubborn and foreign life that each month constructs and then tears down a cradle within it; each month all things are made ready for a child, and then aborted in the crimson flow.*

When we look at menstruation in the light of human imperfection in general, it clearly fits the pattern. As a result of

Adam's sin, man lost the ability to perfect himself, both spiritually and physically. As mentioned earlier, the clearest manifestation of this physical imperfection is man's mortality. Man wears out and dies. The human body does have the innate capability of constantly renewing itself; in theory at least, man has the potential of living forever. This, however, is something that he cannot attain as long as he is in his state of imperfection.

Another large area where human imperfection is evident is in the area of sex and reproduction. One manifestation of this is the menstrual cycle, which is inefficient, uncomfortable, and unesthetic.

Another manifestation of this imperfection is in childbirth itself. Rather than being the natural function that it should logically be, childbirth is often a most traumatic experience. The woman is hospitalized, as if she were experiencing a serious illness, rather than partaking in one of the most natural of bodily functions. The Torah openly states that this is a manifestation of man's imperfection, associated with the sin of Adam and Eve; as God told the first woman (*Genesis 3:16*), "I will increase your anguish in pregnancy—with anguish you shall bear children. . . ." Far from being the natural biological function of continuing the species, pregnancy and childbirth have become painful and anguishing experiences.

A third aspect of the imperfection of man's reproductive process is evident in his general attitude toward sex. Rather than being a simple, natural biological function, sex is the source of man's greatest compulsions and frustrations. There have been many experiments, such as "free sex," which have attempted to "restore" sex to its status as a "natural" human function, but all of these have remained unsuccessful. Man's innate nature demands that he should have psychological conflicts with regard to sex.

One obvious area where man's lack of sexual integration is apparent, is with respect to his attitude toward his body. Of all creatures, man is the only one who experiences shame from his nakedness. This is one of the clearest indications of how Adam's sin affected his entire sexual makeup. Before the

42

sin, the Torah says of man, (*Genesis 2:25*), "The two of them, the man and his wife, were naked, but they were not ashamed." After the sin, however, Adam was to declare (*Ibid. 3:10*), "I was afraid, because I was naked." This change dramatically indicates the fundamental change in man's attitude toward both sex and his body in his degraded state. [38]

Returning to our original discussion, it now becomes obvious why a woman is considered "unclean" when she has her period. This too, is associated with humanity's degraded state and expulsion from Eden. Indeed, our sages openly declare that menstruation is a result of humanity's sin. [39] Therefore, until the woman purifies herself from this ritual uncleanness, she is not allowed to enter the grounds of the Holy Temple, which is a miniature Eden. (This does not apply to going to the synagogue.)

This helps explain why a Niddah is forbidden to have any sexual contact with a man. According to Jewish teachings, sex is not something that is intrinsically shameful or "dirty." Quite to the contrary, it is one of the holiest of all human functions—provided that it is kept within the guidelines of Torah and not perverted. The Hebrew word for marriage is *Kiddushin*, which literally means "sanctification" or "holiness." When a man marries a woman, the words he declares to her are, "Behold you become holy to me with this ring. . . ." [40] Interestingly, the opposite of marriage is prostitution and one of the words for a prostitute is *Kadeshah*— literally, a woman who has defiled her holiness, indicating the "other side" of this holiness, which is its perversion. [41]

One of the reasons sex is so holy is because it has the ability to accomplish something that is beyond the power of any other human function—namely, drawing a soul down to the world, and producing a living human being.

Incidentally, this explains why God's covenant with Abraham involved circumcision—an indelible mark on the organ of reproduction. As the father of the "chosen people," Abraham and his children would now be able to use this organ to bring the holiest souls into the world. Thus, it was only after Abraham circumcised himself that he was able to give birth to Isaac, and it is the sexual organ that bears the mark of God's covenant. [42]

The covenant of circumcision was one of the things that elevated Abraham and his children from the fallen state resulting from the expulsion from Eden. As a result of this covenant, the sexual act of the Jew enters the realm of the holy, and partakes of man's optimum state before his expulsion.

For precisely the same reason that a person who is ritually unclean cannot enter the Holy Temple, a Niddah cannot participate in sexual intercourse. Niddah represents the state of expulsion from Eden. As a result of the covenant of circumcision, however, the sexual act is one of holiness (Kedushah), and therefore, is associated with man's state before the expulsion. Therefore, as long as a woman is in a state of Niddah, she cannot participate in the holy act of sex.

On a simpler level, Niddah is a sign of the imperfection of the human reproductive process. As long as a woman is in a state of Niddah, she may not partake in this reproductive process. [43]

Intercourse between a man, and a woman who is in a state of Niddah is therefore very much like entering the Holy Temple while unclean. Both acts entail entering a representation of man's perfected state while associated with a representation of his fallen state. They both incur the same penalty, namely Korais, being "cut off," as does one who does not enter into the covenant of circumcision. [44]

The punishment of being "cut off" is particularly appropriate for sins such as these. Korais means that the individual is "cut off" from his spiritual source. This spiritual source is very intimately related to Eden. Two major areas where man gains access to his perfected spiritual state is through the Holy Temple and through the covenant of Abraham. Therefore, when a person perverts these vehicles, it is only fitting that he should be cut off completely from his spiritual source.

The punishment of being "cut off" is prescribed as a general punishment for sexual perversions, since all of these are perversions of the covenant of circumcision. [45] Likewise, this is the penalty for violating the Sabbath, Yom Kippur, and Passover, since all of these are times when man is elevated to a state of Eden.

44

This also explains the purification of a Niddah. Since Niddah is associated with the expulsion from Eden, its purification must involve something that re-establishes the connection with Eden, namely, the water of the Mikvah.

This has deeper significance on another level. Earlier, we spoke of how the Mikvah represents the womb, and how it is also connected to the River from Eden. Niddah, however, is a sign of the imperfection of the human reproductive process, especially the womb. Therefore, the purification and rectification of Niddah must be a return to the perfected "womb" that is the Mikvah.

The laws of Niddah, which force man and wife to separate for a period of almost two weeks each month, have the positive function of constantly renewing the sexual bond between them. This, also indicates the imperfection of human sexuality. In essence, this monthly separation is necessary to prevent the couple from becoming bored with sex. To an unmarried person, this may seem farfetched. Nevertheless, according to most marriage counselors, a significant reason for married couples drifting apart is because they simply become bored with each other, and bored with sex. A too common response is for one or both partners to seek sexual liaisons with individuals other than their spouse.

The husband-wife bond is essential for the rearing of human children. On the other hand, the very basic and essential relationship between husband and wife can fall apart through something as undramatic as simple boredom.

In this respect, the laws of Niddah also represent a solution to man's basic sexual imperfection. The monthly separation tends to renew the sexual relationship and thus stabilize the marriage bond. It is interesting to note that among families who observe the Niddah laws, infidelity is virtually unknown, and the divorce rate is significantly below the normal level. In a pragmatic sense, we can say that the structure of the Niddah laws is a system that actually works.

We therefore see that the laws of Niddah have two basic functions. First, the state of Niddah represents the imperfection of man's reproductive process, and therefore, precludes sexual contact until this status is removed through immersion in the Mikvah. On the other hand, it also represents one of the best cures known for this imperfection, which brings about the best possible sexual relationship, stabilizing the fundamental institution of marriage.

On another level, the fact that husband and wife cannot have any physical contact during the days of separation forces them to look upon each other as human beings, rather than as mere sex objects. During this period, they must communicate with each other on a spiritual level, rather than on a mere physical level. "The laws of Niddah insure that for a given period each month, respect, affection and all the other impulses and factors that bind two people, with the exception of the physical, be allowed to dominate the relationship of a married couple. While marriage demands sex, it is much more than sex. Only the Jew has succeeded in abiding by a formula that has made work in practice, the idea that sex is basic to marriage but must be restrained as well as preserved so that other factors could have their due and also that intimacy not become monotonous and unappealing."[46] In this context, the rules of Niddah are most important, since they allow husband and wife to grow together in a manner that would not otherwise be possible. The relationship between man and wife thus grows into a bond that normally cannot exist between man and woman in humanity's imperfect state.

MAN AGAINST NATURE

Another manifestation of man's fallen state is the basic conflict between man and the world around him. Unlike other species whose food is a natural part of their environment, man must toil and work in order to eat. Thus, after man sinned, God told him (*Genesis 3:19*), "by the sweat of your brow, you shall eat bread."

In many respects, metal represents man's ability to destroy nature.[47] Therefore, this too is a basic manifestation of man's lack of harmony with nature. Rather than being a sign of man's perfection, civilization is something that was necessitated by man's lack of natural harmony with nature. His use of metal utensils is therefore also a sign of his expulsion from Eden.

Because of man's fallen nature, he must eat his bread through "the sweat of his brow." He cannot use his intellectual faculties to elevate himself spiritually, but is compelled to use his mind to procure the most basic animal necessities of life. This is particularly evident when man makes use of metal utensils in order to eat and satisfy his animal appetites.

In essence then, just as Niddah represents humanity's basic conflict within its own reproductive process, man's use of metal utensils for eating also represents the conflict of his intellect with respect to another of his natural functions, namely, eating. The Torah therefore states that metal vessels must be (*Numbers 31:23*), "purged with water for a Niddah." Metal vessels must re-establish their harmony with nature through their association with the waters of Eden, just like a Niddah must do so with respect to her sexuality. Like a Niddah, such vessels must be immersed in the Mikvah.[48]

The context in whch the law of immersion of vessels is derived is also very pertinent. The law was declared in the context of a war that Israel fought, which had its beginnings in sexual misconduct between the Jews and the Moabites that ultimately resulted in idolatry. The very fact that man could be tempted into a form of idolatry through sex, indicates that sex is a force that man finds difficult to control, and therefore is a sign of his imperfection. The fact that it can also lead man to wage war and kill, is another sign of his imperfection and inability to live in harmony. The premeditated nature of the battle on the part of the Moabites also underscored the difference between Jew and non-Jew, again a result of man's fall. This entire episode demonstrates that man is not in a perfected state, and that Israel must maintain eternal vigilance if it is ever to return to it.[49]

The spoil that the Israelites brought back from this battle were metal eating utensils—"gold, silver, copper, iron, tin, and lead." That they were obtain through harlotry, idolatry, and killing underscored the fact that these utensils were also indicative of man's fallen state. Therefore, before they could be used, they too, had to be re-elevated through the Mikvah.

We find a similar concept with respect to the giving of the Torah. Here, the Israelites were commanded to immerse in the Mikvah. The wording of the commandment, however, was (*Exodus 19:10*), "they shall wash their garments." As discussed earlier, this meant that they also had to immerse in the Mikvah, since in every instance where the Torah prescribes the washing of clothing, immersion must also be included.

As we have seen, clothing is another sign of man's sin. Before Adam sinned, humanity did not need clothing; people were naked and "not ashamed." Indeed, the very Hebrew word for clothing, *Beged*, comes from the root *Bagad*, meaning "to rebel." Clothing is a sign of man's rebellion against God.

Therefore, since the giving of the Torah represented man's path to his perfected state, it had to be preceded by a "washing of clothing", that is the immersion of the Israelites' clothing (as well as their bodies) in the Mikvah.[50] In this manner, their clothing, which was the very symbol of man's rebellion, was also elevated by the waters of Eden. Only then were the Israelites worthy of receiving the Torah, which is the ultimate instrument of man's return to his perfected state in the World to Come.

*Only a spring and a pit, a gather-
ing of water, shall be clean. . . .*

Leviticus 11:36

WHAT IS A MIKVAH?

The Hebrew word Mikvah means a "pool" or "gathering"
of water.[1] The one place where the Mikvah, as such, is
specifically mentioned in the Torah is in the verse (*Leviticus
11:36*), "Only a spring and a pit, a gathering (*Mikveh*) of
water, shall be clean. . . ." The Torah does not make an
direct statement about what a Mikvah is, nor does it speak of
its use. Nevertheless, as we shall see, all these things are
ultimately included in this verse.

The place, however, where all the rules and laws associated with the Mikvah are enumerated, is in the unwritten or
Oral Torah.[2]

It is important to realize that the Torah consists of two basic
parts. One is the written Torah, the *Torah SheBeKesav*, with
which we are all familiar. This is the Torah scroll that is kept
and read in the synagogue and has been meticulously copied,
generation by generation, from the first Torah written by
Moses.

The second part of the Torah is equally important, even though it is not as well known. It is what we call the Oral or unwritten Torah, the *Torah SheBeal Peh*. This was by and large handed down orally, from master to disciple, for some 1500 years and served as the basis of the Mishnah which was finally put into writing by Rabbi Yehudah the Prince in the beginning of the third cenury c.e. Later this was elaborated upon with discussion and commentary, to form the Talmud. It is from this Oral Torah that all Jewish Law is derived.

The need for an Oral Torah is best illustrated by a simple example. Suppose you want to be a tailor, and I wish to teach you the complexities of how to make men's jackets. There are two ways in which I could go about it. The difficult way would be for me to write a text on making jackets, and then let you try to unscramble a complex set of instructions. A much easier and more logical way would be for me to show you how to make a jacket, and guide you through the various steps. After several such lessons, it would be perfectly clear. A little personal contact can accomplish much more than many books.

The same is true of the Torah. A description of a Mikvah would take many pages, as we shall soon discover. Even then, there would be room for misunderstanding and error. The same would be true of the intricate laws involving such things as Tefillin, Tzitzis, Kashruth, or Sabbath observance. In all these cases, showing how it is done is much simpler and more accurate than trying to describe it. Thus, for example, any observant family knows the basics of how to keep Shabbos. Yet, it takes a keen scholar to master all the written material that tells us how to observe the Sabbath. Things that involve a way of life are taught much more easily by word of mouth and example than by the written word.

This is a possible explanation as to why some of our most common observances are mentioned only in the sparsest terms in the written Torah. There was simply no need for further elaborations, since these things could be best learned by word of mouth and were so commonplace that they could not be forgotten. The things put into writing were often those which were not commonplace and which involved circumstances that would occur only rarely. These had to be detailed in writing, since otherwise the particulars were likely to be forgotten.

A good example of commonplace laws that were not put into writing are those involving Mikvah. Every community had its Mikvah and it was in constant use. This being the case, the details were best preserved orally.

There are six necessary conditions that a body of water must fulfill before it can have the status of a Mikvah.

1. The Mikvah must consist of water. No other liquid can be used.[3]

2. The Mikvah must either be built into the ground, or be an integral part of a building attached to the ground. It cannot consist of any vessel that can be disconnected and carried away, such as a tub, vat, or barrel.[4]

3. The water of a Mikvah cannot be running or flowing. The only exception to this rule is a natural spring, or a river whose water is derived mainly from springs.[5]

4. The water of the Mikvah cannot be drawn, (Sha'uvim). That is, it cannot be brought to the Mikvah through direct human intervention.[6]

5. The water cannot be channeled to the Mikvah through anything that can become unclean, (Tomeh). For this reason, it cannot flow to the Mikvah through pipes or vessels made of metal, clay, or wood.[7]

6. The Mikvah must contain at least 40 Sa'ah (approximately 200 gallons).[8]

It is interesting to see how these laws are alluded to in the Torah. This example will provide us with considerable insight into how the Torah must be analyzed, and how, with proper analysis, it supports the Oral Tradition. (The following discussion is somewhat involved and the casual reader may wish to skip to the next section.)

Since some of the derivations depend on a precise understanding of the words in the verse, it would be useful to present it in the original Hebrew, together with a literal translation:

אַךְ	Ach	Only
מַעְיָן	Ma'yan	a spring
וּבוֹר	U'Bor	and a pit
מִקְוֵה	Mikveh	a gathering
מַיִם	Mayim	of water
יִהְיֶה	yihyeh	[it] shall be
טָהוֹר	tahor	clean. . . .

(Leviticus 11:36)

The Torah was authored by God, and therefore its wording is as precise as an Infinite Intellect could make it. Therefore, there is no word, nuance, grammatical structure, or ambiguity that does not have some significance. Keeping this in mind, we shall see that this verse becomes quite puzzling when we try to analyse each word. We shall therefore introduce a number of questions within the context of these laws and this verse.

Looking at this verse, the first rule is fairly obvious. The Torah clearly states that "a gathering (*Mikveh*) of *water* shall be clean." This excludes all other liquids.[9]

Now let us begin to ask some questions.

Question 1. Why does the verse begin with the word *Ach* (only)? This would appear to be a superfluous word.

There is a tradition that wherever the word *Ach* (only) appears in the Torah, it is meant to be restrictive.[10] To see what it restricts, we must take the verse in context.

Going back two verses, we find that the Torah says (*Leviticus 11:34*), "Any liquid that is drinkable, in any vessel, shall be unclean (if touched by something unclean)." Drinkable liquids, of course, include water, and the Torah states that if they are contained in *any vessel* they can become unclean. The

Torah then says, "Only a spring and a pit, a gathering (*Mikveh*) of waters shall be clean. . . ." From this, it is obvious that the Mikvah cannot consist of any sort of vessel.[11] We thus derive the second rule, that the Mikvah must be built into the ground.

> Question 2. The main point of the verse is that a "gathering (*Mikveh*) of water" is clean. Why is it necessary to specify a spring and a pit?
>
> Question 3. Why are a spring and pit both mentioned? What do we learn from one that we cannot know from the other?

The Torah begins by mentioning a spring. This refers to water that naturally comes from the ground. The word "spring" therefore comes to teach us that the water itself must be completely natural.

The next word, *Bor* or "pit" refers to a hole in the ground, whether or not it is filled with water. An empty hole is also called a *Bor*, as we find (*Genesis 37:24*), "the pit (*Bor*) was empty, there was no water in it."

Furthermore, a *Bor* or "pit" does not have to be natural. It can also be man made, as we find (*Exodus 21:33*), "when a man digs a pit (*Bor*)."

From the word "pit" we learn that the *receptacle* for the Mikvah can be man made. It is only the water that must come in a natural manner.

The first thing we derive from this is the fourth rule, namely, that the water cannot be drawn, or come to the Mikvah through any human intervention.

"Natural water" can consist of water flowing directly from a spring, or more commonly, rainwater. Lake or sea water can also be used. The main restriction is that it not be "drawn" or brought to the Mikvah through human effort.

The receptacle for the water, however, can be man made, the only condition being that it not be a vessel, as mentioned earlier. Included in the category of "receptacle" are any ducts and channels needed to bring the natural water to the Mikvah.[12] We shall explore some of the ramifications of this shortly.

Question 4. Why is the word "gathering" included? The verse should have said, "a spring and a pit of water."

The next word, *Mikveh* or "gathering," indicates that the water must be standing still, "gathered" in one place and prevented from flowing or running. We thus find (*Genesis 1:10*), "the gathering (*Mikveh*) of waters [God] called seas." A "gathering of water" is therefore water than remains in one place, like a "sea."

A Mikvah must be a pool of water in which there is no flow whatsoever. In any case where the water drains from the Mikvah, it is unfit for use, for then it is "flowing" rather than "gathered" water. We thus derive the third rule, that the Mikvah cannot be running or flowing.

Question 5. There is an obvious ambiguity in this verse. It is not clear whether the phrase "a gathering of water" refers just to the pit, or to both the spring and the pit. On one hand, the verse can be read, "a spring, and a pit [which is] a gathering of water." On the other hand, it can also be read, "a spring and a pit [which both are] a gathering of water." What is the reason for this ambiguity?

As we mentioned earlier, everything in the Torah, even ambiguities, must have a reason. The fact that this ambiguity exists indicates that both interpretations are correct.

In one interpretation, the verse reads, "a spring and a pit [which both are] a gathering of water." In this interpretation, the phrase "a spring and a pit" is the modifier, telling us something about "a gathering of water." What it is telling us is that the "gathering of water" must consist of natural water like a spring, but may be in a man made receptacle, like a pit. Thus, "gathering" is the word being modified.

In the other interpretation, the verse reads, "a spring, and a pit [which is] a gathering of water." In this case, the word "gathering" is the modifier, telling us something about the "pit." What it is telling us is that the water in the pit must be a "gathering" and not water that is flowing or leaking. In this interpretation, however, the word "gathering" only refers to "pit" and not to "spring."

From this, we see that the restriction against flowing water only applies to a "pit," but not to a spring.[13] A Mikvah made entirely of natural spring water can be flowing as well as "gathered." If the Mikvah is filled with rain water, however, it cannot be flowing at all. This completes the third rule.

This last rule has important implications with regard to rivers. If the major portion of a river's water comes from underground springs, then the entire river has the status of a spring, and can be used as a Mikvah. If, on the other hand, the river derives its flow primarily from rain water, then it no longer has the status of a spring, and since it is flowing, it is unfit as a Mikvah.[14] Therefore, even though rivers occasionally can be used as a Mikvah, each individual case must be checked by a competent rabbinical expert.

> Question 6. The verb of this sentence, "will be," in the Hebrew is in the singular. Since the sentence contains at least two subjects, "a spring and a pit," why is the plural verb not used?

The singular verb indicates that the "spring and pit" together form a *single* entity called a "gathering of water" or Mikvah. As seen earlier, "spring" refers to the natural water in the Mikvah, while "pit" refers to its man made receptacle. The singular verb teaches us that both of these make up a single entity that is the Mikvah.[15]

This, in turn, would indicate that in order for the Mikvah to be "clean," every element of the receptacle must also be "clean." Therefore, the verse says, "[it] will be clean," using the singular verb.

The only reason water can be brought to the Mikvah through man made ducts and channels is because they are all considered part of the receptacle, and are therefore included in the "pit," which may be man made. If these ducts, channels, or anything else that brings water to the Mikvah, are capable of becoming unclean, then the same will also be true of the pool—and it will no longer have the status of a Mikvah.

From this we learn the fifth rule, namely, that the water cannot be channelled into the Mikvah through anything that can become unclean. The Talmud thus says, " 'It shall be clean'—all of its existence must come about through clean things."[16]

If we now look at the verse carefully, we see that each word teaches us a different law:

Only	*only this, but not a vessel*
a spring	*the water must be natural*
and a pit	*but the receptacle may be man made*
a gathering	*the water cannot be flowing*
of water	*but not any other liquid*
[it] shall be clean	*the receptacle, including all its ducts, must be undefilable*

All six rules are therefore included in this one basic verse. All that it takes to find them is some careful analysis.

There is one final law that we can derive from this verse. Once a pool has the status of a Mikvah, it does not lose this status, no matter what type or how much additional water is added to it.

The Torah says that a Mikvah "shall be clean," in the future tense. This indicates that once a body of water has the status of a Mikvah, there is no way it can become unclean. This is true no matter how much unclean water is poured into the Mikvah.

Therefore, once a pool has the status of a Mikvah, one can add to it as much water as one desires, in any manner whatsoever.

In the Oral Torah, we find that an opening the size of the "neck of a leather bottle" (*Shefoferess HaNod*) is enough to unite two bodies of water into one.[17] According to tradition, this is a hole two finger-widths (approximately two inches) in diameter. If a wall separating two pools contains a hole this size, so that water flows freely from one pool into another, the two pools are considered as one pool.

There is, therefore, another way in which we can add water

to a valid Mikvah. We can build a pool next to it, and leave an adequate hole connecting the two. As soon as the waters of the two pools intermingle, they are considered one, and the water in the second pool is considered to have been "added" to the Mikvah. The second pool, therefore, also becomes a Mikvah. This is the process known as *Hashakah*, which comes from the Hebrew word (*NaShak*), meaning "to kiss."

This is the manner in which most Mikvahs are made. The original Mikvah is a small pool, which is refered to as the *Bor* or "pit," alluding to the "pit" mentioned in the Torah. This is filled with natural rain water, fulfilling the six conditions mentioned earlier. Next to the *Bor* is a larger pool, connected to the *Bor* by an adequate sized hole. This larger pool is filled with ordinary tap water, but as soon as the water covers the hole, the two pools "kiss" and are considered as one. This larger pool than also becomes a Mikvah, and it is generally used for immersion.

One question still remain unresolved. The Torah says that "a spring and a pit, a gathering of water, shall be clean (*Tahor*)." All that the Torah is apparently saying is that the Mikvah itself is ritually clean, but not that it can purify a person. How do we know that it can?

In many places, when the Torah speaks of purification, it simply states, "he shall wash in the water, and he shall be clean."[18] Although no mention is made of Mikvah, we know from the Oral Torah that this washing refers to immersion in the Mikvah.

This can be understood from a relatively simple train of logic. Unless water is in a Mikvah, the water itself becomes unclean when it touches an unclean person. It would not seem logical that water which itself becomes unclean would render a person clean. Therefore, since the only water that cannot become unclean is Mikvah water, this must be the water purification.[19]

When the Torah speaks of ritual purification, the actual words it uses are *U'Rachatz BaMayim*, which literally translated means, "he shall wash in *the* water [and be clean.]" The Torah is not refering to *any* water, but to *the* water—special water. The only water that has a special status with regard to purity is that of the Mikvah.[20]

If there is still any question as to how one washes with the water of a Mikvah, the Torah specifies (*Leviticus 15:16*), "He shall wash *all his flesh* in the water." This clear indicates that the entire body must come in contact with the water of the Mikvah.[21] It is from this that we also learn that there must be nothing intervening between one's body and the water. Any such intervention (*Chatzitzah*) renders the immersion invalid.[22]

The Torah furthermore states with regard to vessels (Leviticus 11:32), "Into the water it shall enter, and it shall be clean." We therefore see that the mode of purification is "entering the water," that is, immersion in a Mikvah. The same is true for a person.[23]

If we look carefully in the Torah, we find that the Hebrew word *Rachatz*— "to wash,"—does not refer to a cleansing process, but rather to purification through water.[24] Therefore, a more accurate translation of *Rachatz* would be "to purify with water," rather than "to wash." Indeed, when we reverse the letters, we see that the word RacHaTz is phonetically very closely related to the word TaHoR, meaning "to purify." Thus, when the Torah says that one should "*Rachatz* in the water," it means that he should "purify himself in the water."

There is one place in the Bible where we clearly see that the meaning of the word *Rachatz* was generally accepted to mean immersion. When Naaman, an Aramanian captain, was struck with leprosy, he went to the prophet Elisha and asked for a cure. The prohet told him (*2 Kings 5:10*), "Go and wash (*Rachatz*) in the Jordan." He was just told to "wash" and nothing more. When Naaman finally took Elisha's advice, however, the Bible states that (*Ibid. 5:14*), "he went down and immersed (*taval*) himself in the Jordan." From this, we clearly see that "*washing*" was generally accepted to mean immersion.[25]

These references from the written Torah reinforce the tradition of the Oral Torah, which is the source of all the laws involving Mikvah.

Next, we must discuss the size of a Mikvah. It obviously

must be large enough for any person to immerse in it.

Like all other rules regarding Mikvah, the precise size is known from the Oral Torah, but at the same time, it is also alluded to in the written Torah. The Talmud derives it from a verse mentioned earlier (*Leviticus 15:16*), "He shall wash all his flesh in the water." The Talmud says that this is "water that takes in all his flesh . . . one *Amah* (cubit) by one *Amah* by three *Amos.*" This, in turn, is said to be equal to 40 *Sa'ah*, (around 25 cubic feet or 200 gallons, as mentioned earlier.)[26]

One of the earlier authorities, Rabbi Yitzchok ben Sheshes (Rivash), explains this Talmudic statement in a most interesting manner.[27] There is a general rule that if something is mixed with twice its volume, it is considered to be nullified.[28] The largest normal human body has a volume of 20 *Sa'ah*. Therefore, the amount of water necessary to "nullify" this body is double this, or 40 *Sa'ah*.[29]

This fits very well with the concept that immersion in a Mikvah involves self nullification and rebirth. We see here, that this is true as a point of Jewish law, as well as from a philosophical viewpoint.

We stated earlier that the Hebrew word *Rachatz*, usually translated as "wash," is more accurately translated as "purify with water." Rabbi Samson Raphael Hirsch points out that it is also phonetically related to the word *Ra'atz*, which means to "overthrow" or "break down."[30] When the Torah speaks of "washing," it is essentially speaking of self-nullification and a "breaking down" of the ego, which is the essence of spiritual purification.

What we have outlined here is a general description of a Mikvah, and not a guide to making one. Those laws are extremely complex and only a rabbinicial expert has the authority to supervise the design and building of a Mikvah.

Steps leading down into the fresh, warm water of a Mikvah

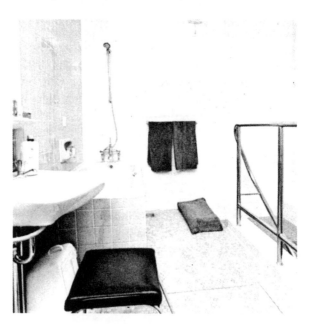

Modern bathroom facilities in the private Mikvah room

THE MYSTERY OF MIKVAH

WATER

Up to this point, we have spoken mostly in symbolic terms. But we have a rule that the commandments, besides having symbolic value, also have profound spiritual effect on man.[1]

Closely linked to this idea is the teaching that everything in the physical world has a spiritual counterpart.[2] Every action in this world likewise has its counterpart in the spiritual realm. The spiritual counterpart of physical man is his divine soul. When man immerses in a physical Mikvah, his soul likewise becomes immersed in its spiritual counterpart. Before we can discuss this, however, let us first understand the spiritual nature of water.

One of the most obvious qualities of water is the fact that it is a liquid. Indeed, in a sense, water is the primary representation of the fluid state.[3] In many instances, when we speak of "water," we are actually speaking of the fluid state in general. Therefore, the spiritual counterpart of water is very closely related to its property of being a fluid.

But what is the main difference between a fluid and a solid? What special property does a fluid have that does not exist in the solid state?

The main difference between them involves change. If only solids were to exist, there would be no change at all. The world would be a dead, airless body in an unchanging frozen state.[4]. For change to be possible, the fluid, as well as the solid state must exist.

If we only have fluids, however, we encounter another problem. Fluids are capable of change, but they do not have any permanence. A fluid will not hold any shape or configuration. If we had a world made only of fluids, there would be change, but no permanence.

Water, being the prototype fluid, is therefore the one substance that primarily represents change and instability. Indeed, when the Torah wants to speak of instability, it uses water as an example, as we find (Genesis 49:4), "Unstable as water."[5]

Life is a unique combination of change and permance. A living thing is constantly changing, and yet, at the same time, it retains its identity. A person constantly undergoes change, and yet, he is still the same person.

Life is also a unique combination of solid and liquid; of course, the most important liquid in living things is water. Water dissolves the nutrients necessary for life, transports them to the various parts of the body, and then does the precise opposite with the body's wastes. Every movement that a living creature makes ultimately involves liquids. All creation contains these two essential spiritual opposites, permance and change, represented physically by solid and liquid. The prototypes of these two states are earth and water respectively.

The Torah describes the world at the beginning of creation by saying, (*Genesis 1:2*), "The earth was formless and chaotic, with darkness on the face of the deep, and God's spirit causing motion on the face of the water." A few questions are immediately raised. Firstly, why is the idea of God's spirit and its connection to the water mentioned at all? Secondly, why is God's spirit primarily associated with water in this passage? Furthermore, the Hebrew word *MeRachefes,* which we translated as "causing motion," has the connotation of both causing motion and caring for something.[6] Why is this particular word used? Finally, why is this word used in the present tense, which seems to take it out of the context of the rest of the verse?

Before answering these questions, however, one thing must be made clear. In describing the six days of creation, the Torah is not attempting to provide us with a scientific description of how the world came into being. The Torah does not try to tell us those things that we can discover through our own intellect or through scientific observation. The Torah places man in perspective to the rest of creation and tells him how to relate to the rest of the universe. The Torah is concerned with the spiritual man and with teaching how the world relates to man with respect to God.

According to many authorities, the "water" mentioned in the first days of creation refers to the fluid state of the universe.[7] Before creation, change did not exist. God dwells in a realm above time, and the concept of change does not apply to Him in any way whatsoever. God thus told His prophet (*Malachi 3:6*), "I am God, I do not change."[8]

Therefore, one of the first ingredients of creation had to be the very concept of change. The newly created universe would be a dynamic, rather than a static entity. But change alone is not enough. Pure change can only result in chaos, and the Torah describes this initial state by saying, "the earth was formless and chaotic."[9]

Left alone, this chaotic fluid state could give rise to anything, good or evil. It was out of this chaotic state that the possibility of evil came into being, and this is alluded to in the next phrase, "and darkness on the face of the deep." This "darkness" is spiritual, rather than a physical,[10] and extended over the "deep," the depths of the "water" not influenced by "God's spirit."

In order for this concept of change to fit into God's general purpose of creation, and bring about sp iritual enlightenment, it would first have to be brought under His constant control. The Torah describes this control by speaking of "God's spirit causing motion on the face of the water." The word, *MeRachefes*, used here also has the connotation of "caring for," since all of God's care for the universe is associated with His guidance of all change and development. This explains why the word *MeRachefes* is in the present tense, indicating that this guidance and providence is constant and continuous.[11]

In the very next verse, the Torah states (*Genesis 1:3*), "And God said, 'Let there be light,' and there was light." After God's providence was established, directing and guiding all change, spiritual enlightenment could be brought to the world.

The Midrash teaches us that this "spirit of God" which was over the waters refers to the "spirit of the Messiah."[12] The Messianic age represents the final fulfillment of God's purpose in creation. It is a time when evil will be vanquished, and good will reign over all mankind. Therefore, the "Spirit of God" that directs all change and movement is a positive force, moving the world toward its ultimate goal of perfection, which is the Messianic Age. (Incidentally, this is *not* in any way meant to identify God with the Messiah.)

On the second day, the Torah tells us that God divided the waters, separating them into the "upper waters" and the "lower waters." The Talmud teaches us that this division was sexual, with the "upper waters" representing the male element, and the "lower waters" representing the female.[13] This is the first place where we find the concept of male and female, representing the two elements of change, of the original "water."

This concept of male and female also alludes to the concept of conception, birth and growth. In giving the waters the attribute of being male and female, God gave them the ability to produce "children." The concept of change would not be haphazard, but would cause development in an organic manner.[14] Ultimately, every concept of "male" and "female" would develop from this.

On the third day of creation, the Torah tells us that God said (Genesis 1:9), "Let the waters under the heavens be gathered together to one place, and let the dry land appear." From the state of "water," that previously constituted the universe, a new concept appeared namely "dry land." In addition to fluidity and change, the concept of solidity and permanence also came into being.[15] This, in turn, would allow for the existence of life, and indeed, we find that the concept of plant life also came into existence on this same third day.

It is on this third day of creation that we see the source of the word Mikvah for the first time. The Torah speaks of the separated water and calls it a Mikveh Mayim—a "gathering of water." The Torah then says (Genesis 1:10), "to the gathering (Mikveh) of waters, He called seas."

The "gathering of water," consisted of the "water under the heavens," which are the "female waters" mentioned earlier. In order for the world to be able to produce life, these waters had to be "gathered to one place", which was called a Mikvah. Ultimately, this original "Mikvah of waters" represented the womb of all life. The scripture alludes to this when it says (Job 38:29,30), "Out of whose womb came the ice. . . the waters which congealed into stone."

We again see water as the concept of change and life in the account of Eden. The Torah says (*Genesis 2:5-7*), "All the bushes of the field had not yet come into being on the earth, and all the grass of the field had not yet grown, for God had not brought rain on the earth. . . . Then a mist rose from the earth, and watered the face of the ground. God then formed man out of the dust of the ground, and blew in his nostrils a soul of life."

Until God brought water to the earth, no life at all, not even plant life, was possible.[16] Man could be formed out of the "dust of the ground" only after water had entered the picture. As the Midrash teaches us, man is a combination of "dust and water," permanence and change.[17] As long as man is alive, this "water" is a most essential part of his being.

In contrast to this, when the Torah speaks of man's death, it says (*Genesis 3:19*), "you are dust, and to dust you shall return." "Earth" and "dust" refer to permanence, while "water" is change. When man is dead, all that is left is permanence— "dust"—since he can no longer grow and change.

The main spiritual concept of water is that of change and development. It represents the growth and development of the world toward fulfilling God's purpose, and, in this context, the Garden of Eden was "watered" spiritually as well as physically. As a result, it was an environment where man could grow and develop according to God's ultimate plan.

The waters of Eden therefore bring together a number of concepts. First of all, these waters represent the "womb" of humanity, since it was with this water that God "formed man of the dust of the earth." Secondly, these waters were the source of the "rivers" that left Eden, which gave man the ability to connect himself with his ultimate source, even in his fallen state, and thus grow toward God's goals.

Most important, we see that water itself represents the change and flow toward God's goal. When a person immerses himself in a Mikvah, he immerses himself spiritually in the basic concept of change itself. Man's ego represents the element of his permanence, and therefore, when he is totally immersed in the concept of change, his ego is nullified. Thus, when he emerges from the Mikvah, he is in a total state of renewal and rebirth.

Water represents two things at the same time. First, it represents change, impermanence and transience. But this very impermanence also means that no evil is ineradicable, and no sin unforgivable. One of the important teachings of Judaism is that repentence can wash away any sin, as the Jerusalem Talmud flatly states, "nothing can stand before repentence.[18] Water therefore also represents the concept of spiritual cleansing.

This is the meaning of the verse (2 *Samuel 14:14*), "We must die, and as waters spilt on the ground, we cannot be gathered up. God does not respect any person, but He devises means so that no one should be banished from before Him." The concept of change is what makes our lives transient, so that we are like "waters spilt on the ground." But this same concept is what God uses to allow all evil to be expiated and forgiven. In essence, the Mikvah represents this spiritual cleansing and renewal.

Through water, everything is ultimately brought back to the fulfillment of God's goal. There may be "darkness on the face of the deep," but "God's spirit is causing motion on the face of the water"—in the present tense, indicating that this is a constant and continuous process. The main vehicle for this is the Torah, which, as our sages teach us, is also a spiritual counterpart of water.[19]

THE MEASURE OF MAN

One of the laws of Mikvah is that it must hold at least forty *Sa'ah*, or approximately 200 gallons of water. In deriving this quantity of forty *Sa'ah*, we saw that in a sense, this was based upon a measure of man.

It is interesting to note that the concept of forty occurs a great many times in the Torah. The Flood of Noah lasted forty days,[20] Moses was on Mount Sinai for "forty days and forty nights" when he received the Torah,[21] and the Israelites similarly spent forty years in the desert.[22] There are many other places where we find the concept of forty in the Bible.[23]

Why is the number forty so important? Why do we come across this number as a duration of time so often in the Torah?

We find the beginnings of an answer in the laws of childbirth, as they applied in the time of the Holy Temple. The pain and infirmity associated with childbirth are an indication of the imperfection of human reproduction, and therefore, they bring about a state of "impurity" in a woman who has given birth. The Talmud states that one reason a woman had to bring a sacrifice after giving birth to a child was because she had so much pain that she would swear never again to bear a child.[24] Childbirth, and the pain associated with it, is related to man's imperfection and therfore requires "purification."

In speaking of this purification, the Torah says (*Leviticus* 12:2,4), "When a woman conceives and bears a male child, she shall be unclean seven days, as the days of Niddah. . . And she shall continue. . . for thirty-three days. . . ." Counting the days required for purificiation after childbirth, we find a total of forty.

Our sages teach us that these forty days represent the time that an embryo takes to attain human form.[25] From a standpoint of Jewish Law, an embryo does not have any status as a human being until forty days after conception.[26] This concept is also sound from a scientific viewpoint, since it is well known that the human embryo beings to assume recognizable human form around the fortieth day after conception.

This helps explain why the flood described in the Torah lasted for forty days. According to the traditional interpretations, the main sin that brought about the flood was sexual immorality. The Midrash thus says that the flood lasted for forty days because the people of that generation "perverted the embryo that is formed in forty days."[27]

It is interesting to note that the Zohar gives a similar reason for the fact that the punishment was through water. The division of the waters represent the original concept of sexuality in creation, with the "upper waters" as the male element, and the "lower waters" as the female. The generation of the flood perverted this basic concept of sexuality, and therefore, the "upper waters" and "lower waters" came together to punish them. The Torah thus says (Genesis 7:11), "The springs of the great deep were split open, and the windows of heaven were opened."[28] This same concept also applies to Mikvah, which can be made up of rain waters and spring waters.

The same concept also applies to the giving of the Torah. This also involves the idea of birth. The Jewish people were born anew under the covenent of the Torah, and the Torah itself, in being transmitted to man, had to undergo a birth process. As in the case of man, this was to take forty days.[29]

The same reasoning also explains why the Israelites spent forty years in the desert. When Moses sent spies to explore the Promised Land, the Torah tells us that (Numbers 13:25), "they returned from spying out the land at the end of forty days." The spies knew that the Israelites would undergo a spiritual rebirth when they entered the Promised Land. In order to experience this rebirth themselves and report on it, the spies spent forty days in the land. They were not worthy of the land, however, and therefore, they brought back a bad report.

As a result of this report, the Israelites rebelled against Moses, not trusting that God would give them the land. It was then decreed that they should spend forty years in the desert, as the Torah says (Numbers 14:34), "Following the number of days in which you spied out the land—forty days—for every day, you shall bear your sins for a year—

forty years." These forty years represent yet another kind of rebirth—the rebirth of an entire generation that would be worthy of eventually entering the Promised Land.

We see that the number forty represents the process of birth. As we have said, it is related to the measure of man. This also explains the forty Sa'ah of water that the Mikvah must contain. The Mikvah also represents the womb, and therefore, these forty Sa'ah parallel the forty days during which the embryo is formed.

In order to understand why birth and embryonic development always involve the number forty, we must introduce yet another concept. Creation consists of four stages, alluded to in the verse (Isaiah 43:7), "All that is called by My Name, for My glory (1), I have created it (2), I have formed it (3), and I have made it (4)." These four stages are represented by the four letters of the Tetragrammaton, God's Name Yud Kay Vav Kay.[30] The first stage is "God's Glory," where things exist conceptually, but not in actuality.[31] The next stage is "creation," which represents creation ex nihilo—"something out of nothing." Then comes "formation" where the primeval substance attains the first semblance of form. Finally comes "making," where the process is completed and yields a finished product.[32]

Our sages also teach us that the world was created with ten sayings.[33] These are the ten times that the expression "and God said" appears in the account of creation.[34] Since these "ten sayings" enter into each of the four stages of creation, the total number of elements of creation is forty.[35] The number forty is therefore very intimately related to the concept of creation.

In enumerating the categories of "work" that are forbidden on the Sabbath, the Talmud teaches us that there are "forty less one."[36] As we know, these thirty-nine categories of "work" parallel the types of activity that went into creation, just as our own Sabbath rest parallels the Sabbath of creation. There is one type of "work," however, that we cannot duplicate, and that is creation ex nihilo—creating something out of nothing. This is the one category that is not included among the types of work forbidden on the Sabbath.

Otherwise, the categories of "work" represent the elements of creation—"forty less one."[37]

The four basic stages that we mentioned earlier are also alluded to in the "four branches" of the river from Eden. As we have discussed, this river is very intimately related to the concept of Mikvah.

The forty Sa'ah of the Mikvah represent the basic elements of creation. The primeval stage of creation was basically one of water. Therefore, when a person passes through the forty Sa'ah of water in the Mikvah, he is passing through the initial steps of creation.

THE LETTER OF TRANSITION

We have seen that Mikvah entails two basic concepts, namely, water and the number forty. Both of these concepts are contained in a single letter, namely, the Hebrew letter *Mem*.

The letter *Mem* derives its name from *Mayim*, the Hebrew word for water. Furthermore, the numerical value of the letter *Mem* is forty. Therefore, it is not very surprising to learn that the letter *Mem* is also said to represent the Mikvah.[38]

Another concept that we find associated with the letter *Mem* is that of the womb.[39] The closed (final) *Mem* is the womb closed during pregnancy, while the open *Mem* is the open womb giving birth.[40] The numerical value forty, associated with *Mem*, then also represents the forty days during which the embryo is formed.

In order to understand the meaning of this letter on a deeper level and see how it relates to Mikvah, we must delve into a most interesting Midrash. The Prophet says (Jeremiah 10:10,) "The Lord, God, is Truth (*Emes*)." The Midrash then gives the following explanation:[41]

> *What is God's seal? Our Rabbi said in the name of Rabbi Reuven, "God's seal is Truth."*
>
> *Resh Lakish asked, "Why is Emes (* אֱמֶת *) the Hebrew word for truth?"*
>
> *He replied, "Because it is spelled Aleph Mem Tav (* אמת *). Aleph (* א *) is the first letter of the Hebrew alphabet, Mem (* מ *) is the middle letter, and Tav (* ת *) is the last letter of the alphabet. God thus says (Isaiah 44:6), "I am first, and I am last."*

From this, we see that the letter *Mem* has a most interesting property. *Aleph*, the first letter of the alphabet, represents the beginning. *Tav*, the last letter, represents the end. *Mem* is the letter that represent transition.

We see this most clearly in the word *Emes* (אֱמֶת) itself. The first two letters, *Aleph Mem* (אם), spell out *Em*, the Hebrew word for mother. This is the beginning of man. The last two letters, *Mem Tav* (מֵת), spell out *Mes*—the Hebrew word for death—the end of man.

72

Most important here, *Mem* represents the concept of transition and change. *Aleph* is the past, and *Tav* the future, so *Mem* represents the transition from past to future. As such, it is the instant that we call the present.

The past is history and cannot be changed. We have no way of even touching the future. Therefore, the arena of action, where all change takes place, is the present. Symbolic of water, the essence of change as well as the number forty, the essence of birth, the letter *Mem* also represents the present—the transition between past and future—which is the arena of all change.

On a deeper level, the transition from past to future also represents an aspect of birth. Indeed, one word for "future" in Hebrew is *HaNolad*, which literally means, "that which is being born."[42] The womb in which the future is born is the present. This is the letter *Mem*.

Thus, when a person enters the Mikvah, he is actually entering the concept of the ultimate present. Past and future cease to exist for him. What he was in the past no longer counts. Even the forty days of formation are no longer an expanse of time, but a volume of water—forty *Sa'ah*.[43] Then, when he emerges from the Mikvah, he reenters the stream of time as if he were a new being.

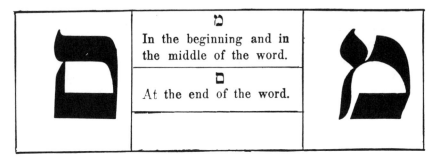

	מ	
	In the beginning and in the middle of the word.	
	ם	
	At the end of the word.	

THE ULTIMATE MIKVAH

> *Rabbi Akiba said: Happy are you, Israel. Before whom do you purify yourselves? Who purifies you? Your Father in heaven! It is thus written (Ezekiel 36:25), "I will sprinkle pure water upon you, and you shall be clean." And it is written (Jeremiah 14:8), "God (HaShem) is Israel's Mikvah." Just as the Mikvah purifies the unclean, so God purifies Israel.*
>
> Mishneh, Yoma 8:9 (85b)

Even though we have delved quite deeply into the concept of Mikvah, Rabbi Akiba's statement still seems quite puzzling. How are we to understand his declaration that "God is Israel's Mikvah?" Furthermore, in this verse, the word *Mikveh* actually means "hope,"and not a Mikvah filled with water, and therfore, the actual translation of the quoted passage is, "God is Israel's hope." What is Rabbi Akiba actually teaching us here?

In order to find the answer to this question, we must first understand the significance of God's name. In the Torah, we find that God is most usually called by two names. The first is *Elokim*, usually translated as "God." The second is the Tetragrammaton, which we read as *Ad-noy* or *HaShem,* and often translate as "the Lord" or "the Eternal." Each one of these Names has a very special significance.

The Name *Elokim* represents God as the Ruler of the universe. The same word—*Elokim*—is therefore also used for judges and angels. [44] We interpret *Elokim* to mean "master of all power," indicating God's relationship to the universe, constantly interacting with it and giving it existence. [45] When the Name *Elokim* is used to express God's relationship to man, it indicates that He is acting with strict justice. [46]

The Name *Hashem,* on the other hand, represents God as the ultimate source of all existence, high above the universe and its laws. [47] We interpret this Name as indicating that God, "was, is, and will be." [48] It speaks of Him as existing completely beyond the realm of space and time. Past and future are exactly the same as the present for God, and indeed, He sees the entire expanse of time in a single glance." [49] Thus, when we make use of the Name *HaShem*, we are really saying that God, "was, is, and will be" all at once. Past and future are exactly the same as the present for Him.

The Name *HaShem* is also associated with God's attribute of mercy. [50] This, however, is closely related to the concept of His existence outside of time.

One of the most important teachings of Judaism is that of repentence. No matter how great a sin a person might have committed, his slate can be wiped completely clean if he sincerely repents before God. This, in essence, is also the concept of God's mercy.

There is, however, a very difficult question associated with the idea of repentence. Let us say that a person committed murder, or did some other irreparable harm. How can his repentence undo the damage that has already been done? We can see, perhaps, how the sin can be forgiven, but how can the slate be wiped completely clean?

The author of *Sefer HaIkkarim* provides us with a very profound answer to this question. [51] The guilt for every wrongful deed is very dependent upon the motivation accompanying it. For example, there is a great difference between an individual who kills another person out of hate, and one who does so accidentally. Indeed, there are times when killing can be justified and virtuous, such as when it is necessary to stop a would be murderer. [52] There are many conceivable motivations that could mitigate acts which would otherwise be considered sinful.

Therefore, although the damage itself cannot be undone, the motive can be reappraised. When a person repents, he regrets his wrongdoing, and his repentance now is counted as his motive when he did this wrong. The Talmud thus teaches us that, "repentence is great, since it can make purposeful sins to be counted as accidental ones." [53]

Still, this answer does not remove the difficulty completely. How can my regret at this moment be transfered to a deed that I did a long time ago? How do we remove the barrier of time that separates the regret and the deed?

We, of course, cannot do this, since we are bound by time. But God can. God is completely outside of time, and, therefore, He can simply overlook the time barrier between the deed and the regret, and count the two together.

This is the concept of God's mercy. In erasing sin, God is above time, bringing past and present together. Both of these concepts—God's mercy and His existence outside of time—are contained in His Name *HaShem*. [54]

On a deeper level, the Name *HaShem* indicates that God is observing man from a perspective outside of time. He is judging the individual with respect to his future as well as his past, as well as in the context of the entire past and future of all creation.

We therefore see that when we use the Name *HaShem*, we are indicating that God is the ultimate present. Through this Name, which indicates "was, is, and will be"—all at once—both the past and future are also included in the present.

In this context, there is no difference between past, present and future. Just as the present can be altered and rectified, so can the past—and even the future. This represents the ultimate freedom. As long as a person is bound to the concept of *HaShem*, he is free of both the past and the future.

As we mentioned earlier, the Mikvah is connected to the concept of the letter *Mem*, which represents the present. The Name *HaShem*, however, draws everything into the present even the past and the future. It is a spiritual level where past, present and future are one, and where the evil of the past can be expiated by the regret of the present.

This is the meaning of Rabbi Akiba's declaration that "Ha-Shem is Israel's Mikvah." Just as Mikvah represents the present, the Name *HaShem* represents a concept where the "present" even includes the past and future. Therefore, *HaShem* is the ultimate Mikvah. [55]

As we have pointed out, however, the word *Mikveh* in this context is actually more properly translated as "hope." How is this related to the Mikvah of water? The verse itself indicates this relationship, since it says (*Jeremiah* 17:13), "God (*HaShem*) is Israel's hope (*Mikvah*). All who forsake You shall be ashamed (dried up). . . because they have forsaken God, the Fountain of living waters."

Why does the Hebrew language use the same word for hope as for Mikvah?

But what is hope? It actually represents our feelings toward an event in the future. When we hope that some future event will happen, we are dealing with something that is beyond the barrier of time. We therefore say that our hope is *HaShem*—the Name that we use when we speak of God as existing outside of time. For *HaShem*, there is no barrier between present and future, and therefore, when we associate with Him, our hope can likewise pierce the barriers of time. Therefore, hope, like the concept of Mikvah, is that which places us outside the limitations of time. In both cases, we do so through the power of HaShem.

As we know, the word Mikvah actually means a *"gathering."* Taken in this context, it is also a gathering of time—a gathering of past and future into the present, making them both accessible to us.[56]

On a simpler level, as discussed earlier, the concept of Mikvah is related to that of self negation. When a person places all his hope in God, however, this in itself is a profound negation of one's ego.

Rabbi Samson Raphael Hirsch writes that the Hebrew word *Tumah*, which we usually translate as "unclean," belongs to a phonetic family of words relating to the lack of freedom and independence.[57] Thus, all things associated with ritual uncleanness are things that indicate man's lack of freedom. Of all these, death is the ultimate, since it represents man's ultimate subjugation to the laws of nature.

The ability to transcend the bonds of time, on the other hand, is the ultimate freedom. Therefore, when a person enters the Mikvah, he enters a state where past, present and future are "gathered together," and is therefore utlimately free. He is no longer bound by either past or future, but exists in an absolute present, which is the one instant of time over which man has control. Therfore, the freedom of Mikvah overcomes the lack of freedom associated with *Tumah*.

Ultimately then, all purification comes from God's unity, which extends into time as well as every other aspect of existence. God's unity in time is precisely what we have been discussing, that He is one and the same in past, present and future, and therfore, conversely, past, present and future are all the same to Him.

This is the ultimate concept of the purification of the Mikvah. The scripture speaks of this when it says, (*Job 14:4*), "Who can bring the clean out of the unclean, if not the One?"[58]

NOTES

INTRODUCTION

1. *Cf. Turey Zahav (Taz), Yoreh Deah* 268:8.
2. See *Biur Halachah, Orech Chaim* 468:4 *"VeChomrey."*
3. See Rashi, *Yoma* 67b *"Chok,"* Rashi, Ramban, on Numbers 19:1, *BaMidbar Rabbah* 19:1, *Pesikta* 4 (40b). The root of this word is *Chokek,* meaning "to rule" or "to decree," *cf.* Genesis 29:10, Numbers 21:18, Judges 5:9, Isaiah 33:22. For a general discussion of the three categories, see *Yoma,* 67b, *Sifra* on Leviticus 18:4, Rashi on Genesis 26:5, Leviticus 18:4, 20:26; Rambam, *Shemonah Parakim* #6, *Yad, Meilah* 8:8; Ramban on Leviticus 16:8, Deuteronomy 6:20; Radak on 1 Kings 2:3; *Emunos VeDeyos* 3:2 (54a), *Kuzari* 2:48 (55a), *Ikkarim* 1:17.
4. *Yad, Mikvaos* 11:2, *Chinuch* 159. See note 11.
5. *Yoma* 67b.
6. *Shabbos* 68a.
7. *Ibid.*
8. Rashi *ad loc. Cf. Sifra* on Leviticus 20:26, Rambam, *Shemonah Perakim* #6, *Chayay Adam* 68:18. Also see Maharitz Chayos on *Rosh HaShanah* 16a, Rambam on *Makkos* 3:16, *Chovos HaLevavos* 3:3.
9. *Yad, Tumas Ochlin* 16:8, *Moreh Nebuchim* 3:47, *Kuzari* 3:49 (55a). See Numbers 19:13,20.
10. *Yad, Mikvaos* 1:1–3. Also see *Pesachim* 16a, *Sefer HaMitzvos,* postive commandment 109.
11. *BaMidbar Rabbah* 19:8, *Tanchuma Chukas* 8, *Pesikta* 4 (40b). See *Megilas Esther* (on *Sefer HaMitzvos*) positive commandment 96.
12. *Yad, Temurah* 4:13, *Tshuvah* 3:14, *Mikvaos* 11:12; *Moreh Nebuchim* 3:27, 3:31; Ramban on Leviticus 19:19, Deuteronomy 22:6, *Chinuch* 545, Ibn Ezra on Exodus 20:1, *Tosefos Tom Tov* on *Berachos* 5:3, *Etz Yosef* on *VaYikra Rabbah* 27:10, *Devarim Rabbah* 6:1, Maharitz Chayos on *Sotah* 14a. *Cf. Tosefos, Sotah* 14a, *Chulin* 5a *"Kedey,"* *Gittin* 49b *"R. Shimon,"* Maharam *ad loc., Tosefos Yom Tov* on *Sanhedrin* 8:6, 10:5. Also see *Baba Kama* 79b, *Baba Metzia* 3a, *Milchamos HaShem* (Ramban), *Rosh HaShanah* (Rif 11a) "VeOd."
13. *Yerushalmi Nazir* 7:2 (35a), Maharam Di Lanzano, *Shiurey Karban, ad loc., Shiltey Giborim, Avodah Zarah* (Rif 6a) #1, *Shnei Luchos HaBris, Torah SheBaal Peh, K'lal Drushim VeAgados* (Jerusalem 5720) 3:241a, *Terumos HaDeshen* 108, *Shiurey Berachah, Yoreh Deah* 183:1.
14. *Yad, Mikvaos,* 11:2, *Sefer HaChinuch* 175.
15. Exodus 29:4, *Targum J.,* Rashi, Hirsch *ad loc. Cf.* Exodus 40:12, Leviticus 8:6.
16. Leviticus 16:4, 24, *Targum J.,* Rashi *ad loc., Yoma* 3:3, 4 (30a), 3:6 (34b), 7:3, 4 (70a). *Cf.* Rabbi Nathan of Nemerov, *Likutey Halachos (Yoreh Deah) Hechsher Kelim* 4:33.
17. Rashi, *Yebamos* 47b *"Sham Ger."* See, however, Rashba *Ibid.*
18. *Yebamos* 47b. Note that the basic act of purification is *emerging* from the Mikvah, see *Kesef Mishneh, Avos HaTumah* 6:16, *Makor Chesed* (on *Sefer Chasidim*) 394:3. *Cf.* Ran, *Nedarim* 76b (top) *"U'Mehadrin,"* *Tosefos, Shabbos* 35a *"VeYarad."*

19. *Yebamos* 22a, 48b, 62a, 97b, *Bechoros* 47a, *Tosefos, Sanhedrin* 71b *"Ben,"* *Yad, Edos* 13:2, *Issurey Biah* 14:11.

20. *Reshis Chochmah, Shaar HaAhavah* 11 (New York, 5728) 92b. [From a Kabbalistic viewpoint, Mikvah is associated with the Name *Ekyeh* (I Will Be), which, when "filled" with the letters *Heh*, adds up to 151, the numerical equivalent of Mikvah. *Shaar HaKavanos, Inyan Tevilah Erev Shabbos* (Ashlag, Tel Aviv 5722) p. 25, *Shaar Ruach HaKodesh* (Ashlag, Tel Aviv 5723) p. 36, *Shnei Luchos HaBris, Shaar HaOsios, Kedushah* 1:168a, *Shaarey Gan Eden, Shaar HaOsios, Mem* (95a), *Keser Shem Tov #2, Sefer Baal Shem Tov, Yisro* 11, *Pri HaAretz* (Menachem Mendel of Vitebsk) on *Lech Lecha;* HaGra on *Tikuney Zohar* 19 (37a) *"Inun,"* *Likutey Halachos (Yoreh Deah) Melichah* 1:4. This Name, however, is associated with the womb of *Binah,* see *Etz Chaim, Shaar Huledes Abbah Velmah* 3(1:236), *Shaar HaY-ereach* 3(2:176), *Adir BaMarom* 90a. Mikvah is also associated with the Name *ELeD,* which literally means "I will be born." *Keser Shem Tov, loc. cit.*]

21. *Ohalos* 7:4, 5 *Chulin* 4:3 (71a), *Yad, Tumas Mes* 25:12.

22. *Sefer HaChinuch* 173, *Likutey Halachos (Yoreh Deah) Nedarim* 2:11, *Mikvah* 1:1, *Hechshar Kelim* 4:12; *Dover Tzedek* (R. Tzaduk of Lublin) p. 7b; Hirsch on Exodus 29:4, Leviticus 11:47. See *Berashis Rabbah* 4:1, 5:2, *Yerushalmi Chagigah* 2:1 (8b), *Zohar Chadash* 12a, Rashi on Genesis 1:1, Psalm 104:3.

23. *Yalkut Shimoni* 1:3 (on Genesis 1:8), *Keses HaSofer* (R. Aaron Marcus) on Genesis 1:2, *Likutey Halachos (Yoreh Deah) Mikvah* 1.

24. *Chulin* 89a.

25. *Likutey Halachos loc. cit.* 1:1, *Dover Tzedek loc. cit.*

26. *Yoma* 85a, *Bechoros* 46b, from Genesis 7:22.

27. *Likutey Halachos (Yoreh Deah) Hechshar Kelim* 4:20 (143c).

28. *Likutey Halachos, loc. cit.* 4:18,38. Cf. Proverbs 30:16.

29. *Shabbos* 129a, *Niddah* 21a, *Ohalos* 7:4.

30. *Sifra* on Leviticus 11:36.

31. *Terumos* 9:7, *Maasros* 5:2, *Pesachim* 34a, *Yerushalmi Maasros* 5:1 (22b), *Sifra* on Leviticus 11:38, *Yad, Tumas Ochlin* 2:19, *Kesef Mishneh ad loc.*

WHEN THE MIKVAH IS USED

1. Rashi on Leviticus 15:19, *Targum* on Leviticus 12:12, 15:19, Rashbam, Bachya, Hirsch, on Leviticus 12:12, Ibn Ezra on Numbers 19:9, Radak on Isaiah 30:22; Rashi, *Shabbos* 64b *"BeNidasa."*

2. *Sefer HaMitzvos,* negative commandment 348.

3. Leviticus 20:17, *Sefer HaMitzvos,* negative commandment 331.

4. Exodus 12:15, 19, Leviticus 23:29, 31, *Sefer HaMitzvos,* negative commandments 196, 197.

5. *Zohar* 2:142b, *Nefesh HaChaim* 1:18, *Likutey Amarim (Tanya)* 3:5 (95b), *Or HaChaim* on Leviticus 17:10. For further discussion, see *Emunos VeDeyos* 9:9 (88a), Ramban on Leviticus 15:31, 18:29, *Shaar HaGamul* 78a, from

Rosh HaShanah 17a, Bachya on Genesis 18:25, Abarbanel on Numbers 15:23.

6. *Sanhedrin* 90b, *Makkos* 13b, *Yad, Tshuvah* 6:2, Rashi on Numbers 15:31, *Prin Megadim*, introduction to *Orech Chaim* 3:19.

7. *Targum J. ad loc., Torah Temimah* on Leviticus 15:33. *Cf. Yad, Issurey Biah* 4:3, 11:16, from Leviticus 15:18, *cf. Sifra ad loc.* A Niddah is in the same category as a *Zav*, and therefore, her purification is the same, *cf.* Ramban on Leviticus 15:23. The *Gaonim* derive this immersion logically from the fact that even the things that a Niddah touches must be immersed, see *Tosefos, Yebamos* 47b *"BaMakom," Chagigah* 11a *"Lo Nitzracha," Yoma* 78a *"MiKan," Sefer Mitzvos Gadol (Smag),* positive commandment 248, *Hagahos Maimoni* on *Yad, Issurey Biah* 4:3, Bachya on Leviticus 15:19.

8. Rashi, *Yebamos* 47b *"Chotzetz."* Cf. *Kuzari* 3:49 (55a).

9. *Avodah Zarah* 75b, Tosefos loc. cit.

10. Radak *ad loc., Yoma* 78a, *Yerushalmi Shekalim* 6:2 (26a), Hirsch on Numbers 31:23.

11. *Niddah* 31b. This, however, is not the only reason, and therefore, the laws of Niddah apply equally well to an unmarried girl. See *Sefer HaChinuch* 95, *Toras HaShelamim* (on *Yoreh Deah*) 183:4, *Tiferes Yisroel* (*Keresei U'Plesei*) 183:3, *Darkey Tshuvah* (on *Yoreh Deah*) 183:13.

12. *Yoreh Deah* 183:1 in *Hagah.*

13. *Shaarey Tshuvah* (R. Yonah) 3:95.

14. *Tshuvos Rivash* 425.

15. *Targum J.,* Rashi, Ramban, *ad loc., Sotah* 37b, *Shavuos* 37a. See Joshua 8:33, 34.

16. *Shavuos* 29a, Maharsha *ad loc. "KeSheHishbia,"* Rashash *ibid., Nedarim* 25a. Also see *Nedarim* 8a, *Nazir* 4a, *Yad, Nedarim* 3:7, *Shavuos* 11:3, *Shach, Yoreh Deah* 119:22, HaGra, *Yoreh Deah* 228:99, Maharitz Chayos on *Nedarim* 8a, *Nazir* 4a.

17. *Kerisus* 9a, *Yad, Issurey Biah* 13:1.

18. See Exodus 12:48, Joshua 5:5, *Yebamos* 71b. Also see Radal (on *Pirkey DeRabbi Eliezer*) 29:1, 49; Ramban, Rashba on *Yebamos* 46a *"SheKen."*

19. *Mechilta,* Ramban *ad loc., Yebamos* 46b, *Yad, loc. cit.*

20. Radak, Abarbanel *ad loc.*

21. *Kerisus* 9a, *Yad, Issurey Biah* 13:4.

22. *Yebamos* 46b, Tosefos *ad loc. "Mishpat," Yad, Issurey Biah* 13:6, *Yoreh Deah* ·268:3, *Shach ad loc.* 268:8, 9.

23. *Sifri* (32) on Deuteronomy 6:5, *Avos DeRabbi Nathan* 12:8, *Berashis Rabbah* 39:14, *BaMidbar Rabbah* 14:1, Rashi on Genesis 12:5.

24. *Berashis Rabbah* 84:4, Bachya on Genesis 12:5.

25. *Zohar* 1:102b. *Cf. Sifra,* Rashi, on Leviticus 15:11, *Yad, Mikvaos* 1:2. Also see *Shaar Ruach HaKodesh* p. 36.

26. Rashi on Genesis 18:4, *Baba Metzia* 86b.

27. *Avodah Zarah* 5:12 (75b), *Yad, Maachalos Issuros* 17:3, *Yoreh Deah* 120.

28. *Yerushalmi, Avodah Zarah* 5:15 (37b). *Cf. Torah Temimah* on Numbers 31:23 #32.

29. *Yoreh Deah* 121:1.

30. *Yoreh Deah* 120:3, Meiri, *Avodah Zarah* 75b, Rosh, *Pesachim* 1:10, Mordecai, *Pesachim* 538, *Avodah Zarah* 849 (note).

31. In *Yad, Maachalos Issuros* 17:5, this is called a law from *Divrey Sofrim*. In general, the Rambam uses this expression to denote any law that is derived from the Oral Torah, see *Sefer HaMitzvos, Shoresh* 2 (26b), *Kesef Mishneh* on *Ishus* 1:2. Therefore, we find that *Tshuvos Rashba* 3:255, quoted in *Bais Yosef, Yoreh Deah* 120 (191b), maintains that the Rambam takes it to be a Torah law, *cf. Lechem Mishneh ad loc.* However, see Ran, *Avodah Zarah* (Rif 39b) "*Mishkanta*" who writes that the Rambam takes it to be a rabbinical law, see Meiri, *Avodah Zarah* 75b, Radbaz, *Kesef Mishneh*, on *Yad, loc. cit. Terumas HaDeshen* 156 *(quoted in Bais Yosef, loc. cit.)* and Raavad (quoted in Ran, *loc. cit.* and *Toras HaBayis* 4:4) maintain that it is a Torah law, *cf. Chidushey Hagahos* on *Tur, Yoreh Deah* 120:6, Meiri, *Avodah Zarah* 75b. Ramban on Numbers 31:23, writes that it is a rabbinical law, *cf.* Hirsch on Leviticus 11:32. *Tosefos*, quoted in notes 7 and 9, however, clearly must hold it to be a Torah law.

32. *Sifri ad loc., Avodah Zarah* 75b, *Orech Chaim* 451:4.

33. *Targum J.*, Rashi, Ibn Ezra, Ramban, *ad loc., Avodah Zarah* 75b.

34. *Berachos* 55a, *Chagigah* 27a, *Minachos* 97a, *Orech Chaim* 167:5 in *Hagah, Magen Avraham* 180:4. See Ezekiel 41:22.

35. Hirsch on Numbers 31:23.

36. *Cf. Zebachim* 9:7 (86a), 87a, from Exodus 30:29, *Yad, Pesuley HaMikdashin* 3:18.

37. *Yoreh Deah* 268:12 in *Hagah,* 267:8 in *Hagah, Taz* 267:5, *Magen Avraham* 326:8, *Machatzis HaShekel ad loc.; Nimukey Yosef, Yebamos* (Rif. 16b) "*Kidushav,*" *Maharil, Erev Yom Kippur* (44a), *Avos DeRabbi Nathan* 8:8. Also see *Tshuvos HaGaonim (Shaarey Tzedek)* 3:6:8 (24b), *Tshuvos Rashba* 5:6, *Makor Chesed* (on *Sefer Chasidim*) 203:1.

38. Mordecai, *Yoma* 723, Rosh 8:24, *Rokeach* 214, *Sefer Chasidim* 394, Abudraham, *Erev Yom Kippur* (p. 279), *Maharil loc cit., Menoras HaMaor* 5:2:2:1 (295), from *Pirkey DeRabbi Eliezer* 46; *Orech Chaim* 606:4, *Taz* 606:5, *Beer Hetiv* 606:68, *Tshuvos Chavas Yair* 181.

39. *Orech Chaim* 581:4 in *Hagah; Kol Bo* 64 (p. 27a).

40. *Zohar* 2:204a, *Yesod VeShoresh HaAvodah* 8 (Jerusalem 5725) p. 213, *Shaar HaKavanos* 2:25, *Shnei Luchos HaBris* 1:167a.

41. *Sefer Chasidim* 394, *Rokeach* 214 (p. 103), *Shnei Luchos HaBris* 1:167a, *Maharil loc. cit., Magen Avraham* 606:8, *Taz* 606:5. The three times are Genesis 1:10, Exodus 7:10, and Leviticus 11:36. God is also called the "Mikvah" of Israel in three places, Jeremiah 14:8, 17:13, 50:7.

A DEEPER LOOK

1. *Emunos Ve Deyos* 1:4 (end), 3:0, *Sefer HaYashar* 1, *Pardes Rimonim* 2:6, *Etz Chaim, Shaar HaKelalim* 1, *Reshis Chochmah, Shaar HaTshuvah* 1, *Shnei Luchos HaBris, Bais Yisroel* 1:21b, *Shomrei Emunim (HaKadmon)* 2:13, *Derech*

Ha Shem 1:2:1. See *God, Man and Tefillin*, p. 35.

2. This entire discussion is taken from *Derech HaShem* 1:2.

3. Cf. *Mechilta* on Exodus 14:29, *Berashis Rabbah* 21:5, *Shir HaShirim Rabbah* 1:46, *Yad, Tshuvah* 5:1.

4. *Derech HaShem* 1:2:2. Cf. *Midrash Tehillim* 26:3, 36:4, *Reshis Chochmah, Shaar HaYirah* 7 (22b); *Sanhedrin* 39b, *Berashis Rabbah* 9:12–14. See Isaiah 45:7, *Derech HaShem* 1:5:8; *Bahir* 13, *Moreh Nebuchim* 3:10, *KaLaCh Pischey Chochmah* 39 (24b). Also see *Akedas Yitzchok* 70 (3:145b), *Etz Chaim, Shaar HaMelachim* 5, *Sefer Baal Shem Tov, Sh'mos* 9.

5. *Chulin* 60b. Cf. *Shefa Tal* (Brooklyn 5720) 2c.

6. *Targum J.* on Genesis 2:15, *Yalkut ad loc.* 22, *Sifri* on Deuteronomy 11:33, Alshich, Bachya, *ad loc.*

7. *Kiddushin* 4:14 (82a).

8. *Nefesh HaChaim* 1:5 (6a), note: "*VeHaInyan.*" Cf. *Zohar* 1:35b.

9. *Ibid.*

10. *Ibid.* 7a. Cf. *Abarbanel ad loc., Berashis Rabbah* 16:6. Also see *Avodah Zarah* 5a, *Avodas HaKodesh* 2:21 (41d).

11. *Berachos* 5a, *Succah* 52a, *Kiddushin* 30a, *Zohar* 1:190a, 3:268a.

12. See *Adir BaMarom* 11a.

13. *Kiddushin* 30b, *Sifri* on Deuteronomy 11:18; *Baba Basra* 16a.

14. *BaMidbar Rabbah* 13.2, *Shir HaShirim Rabbah* 5:1, *Pesikta Rabosai* 5 (18b).

15. *Yad, Tumas Ochlin* 16.8, *Moreh Nebuchim* 3:47, *Kuzari* 3:49 (55a).

16. Rashi on Numbers 19:13, Shavuos 16b; *Sifra*, Rashi, on Leviticus 17:16, *Yad, Biyas HaMikdash* 3:12.

17. Cf. *Yad, Mikvaos* 11:12, *Shnei Luchos HaBris, Shaar HaOsios, Taharah* (1:108a).

18. *Derech HaShem* 1:5:9, 4:6:2, *Kav HaYashar* 17. See Leviticus 16:30, Jeremiah 33:8, Ezekiel 14:11, 20:43, 36:7, Psalm 51:4, Proverbs 20:9, Job 4:17. In particular, Tumah is associated with sexual immorality, and indeed this is the first context in which we find the word in the Torah in Genesis 34:5. Also see Leviticus 18:24, Numbers 5:13, 14, 27, 28, Ezekiel 18:6, 22:11, Hoseah 5:3, 6:10.

19. Cf. Numbers 19:13 *ff.*, Leviticus 11:8, 24, 31, 39, 21:1. See Alshich on Leviticus 21:1.

20. Alshich, *loc. cit., Likutey Halachos (Yoreh Deah) Mikvaos* 1:1.

21. *Alshich loc. cit.* Cf. *Zohar* 3:47a, 3:79a.

22. *Bechoros* 55a. See Malbim on Genesis 2:10.

23. *Pirkey DeRabbi Eliezer* 20 (47b).

24. Midrash, quoted in *Yalkut Reuveni* on Genesis 2:10 (31b); *Likutey Halachos (Yoreh Deah) Giluach* 4:16, *Hechshar Kelim* 1:2. Cf. *Shaarey Orah* 8 (83b), that this river is *Binah*, which is also associated with Mikvah. See Jeremiah 31:8, *Tikuney Zohar* 12a. See *BaMidbar Rabbah* 18:21, where the Midrash derives the fact that a Mikvah must contain 40 Sa'ah from (Isaiah 8:6), "The waters of Shiloach, that go slowly *(L'at).*" The numerical value of the word *L'at* is 40. Shiloach, however, is identified with Gichon, one of the rivers from Eden, *cf. Targum J.* on 1 Kings 1:33, 38, 45, Rashi, *Berachos* 10b, "*Sasam,*" Radal on *Pirkey DeRabbi Eliezer* 20:30.

25. *Tikuney Zohar* 19 (39a), *Kisey Mlech* (61b #2). HaGra, *ad loc., Shnei Luchos HaBris, Shaar HaOsios, Kedushah* 1:166b, *Sefer Baal Shem Tov, Yisro* 11.
26. *Derech HaShem* 1:3:5, 1:3:8, 2:4:2, 2:4:6, *Adir BaMarom* 11a.
27. *Avos* 5:2.
28. *Sh'mos Rabbah* 30:13, Maharzav on *Berashis Rabbah* 32:5.
29. *Cf. Berachos* 7b, *Sotah* 10b, *Berashis Rabbah* 31:21, Rashi on Genesis 12:5, Maharitz Chayos on *Chagigah* 3a. Also see *Yalkut* 1:766, *Yoma* 28b, *Yad, Avodas Kochavim* 1:3.
30. *Zohar* 1:75a, Alshich on Genesis 11:1.
31. *Derech HaShem* 2:4:3.
32. *Sifri*, Bachya, Alshich, *Or HaChaim, ad loc.*
33. *Avodah Zarah* 2b, *Mechilta* on Exodus 20:2, *Sifri, Targum J.*, Rashi, Ramban, on Deuteronomy 33:2, *Sh'mos Rabbah* 27:8, *BaMidbar Rabbah* 14:22, *Eichah Rabbah* 3:3, *Tanchuma, Yisro* 14, *Shoftim* 9, *Zos HaBeracha* 4; *Pirkey DeRabbi Eliezer* 41 (95b), *Pesikta* 29 (186a), *Zohar* 2:3a, 3:192b.
34. See "When Mikvah is used," note 20.
35. *Cf. Likutey Halachos (Yoreh Deah) Avadim* 2:9.
36. *Likutey Halachos (Yoreh Deah) Niddah* 1:3, *Giluach* 4:16, *Mikvah* 1:1. See Zechariah 14:8, Bachya on Numbers 19:16.
37. Bantam Books, New York 1970, p. 25.
38. Abarbanel *ad loc.*, Rashi Sforno, Alshich, on Genesis 2:25, *Moreh Nebuchim* 1:2, *Reshis Chochmah, Shaar HarKedushah* 16 (196b).
39. *Shabbos* 32a, *Eruvin* 100b, *Yerushalmi, Shabbos* 2:6 (20a), *Berashis Rabbah* 17:8, *Tanchuma, Metzorah* 9.
40. *Kiddushin* 2b. *Cf. Tosefos ad loc. "deAssar."*
41. Rashi, *Sanhedrin* 82a "*Kodesh,*" Rashi, Rashbam, on Genesis 38:21, Rashi, Ibn Ezra, Hirsch, on Deuteronomy 23:18. *Cf.* 1 Kings 14:24, 15:12, 22:47, 2 Kings 23:7, Hoseah 4:14, Job 36:14.
42. *Tiferes Yisroel* (Maharal) #2. *Cf. VaYikra Rabbah* 27:10, *Derech Mitzvosecha* (Chabad) p. 9b.
43. *Likutey Halachos (Yoreh Deah) Niddah* 2:7.
44. Genesis 17:14, *Kerisos* 1:1 (2a), *Yad, Milha* 1:1.
45. *Cf.* Leviticus 18:29, *Kerisos* 2b, *Yad, Issurey Biah* 1:1, *Sefer HaMitzvoz,* negative commandment 352.
46. *THE ROAD TO RESPONSIBLE JEWISH ADULTHOOD,* by Rabbi Pinchas Stolper, page 12.
47. *Cf. Sanhedrin* 76b, *Midos* 3:4, *Berashis Rabbah* 5:10, *Mechilta,* Rashi, Ramban, on Exodus 20:22. Metal also represents the concept of money and commerce, *cf. Baba Metzia* 4:1, *Likutey Halachos (Yoreh Deah) Hechshar Kelim* 3:3.
48. *Likutey Halachos, loc. cit.* 1:2.
49. *Ibid.* 4:13.
50. *Cf.* Alshich on Leviticus 14:8. The main concept of clothing is wool and linnen (*Shabbos* 26b, *Yebamos* 4b, *Minachos* 39b). Since these have no place in water, everything in the sea is clean. *Cf. Sifra* on Leviticus 13:48, Bertenoro on *Negaim* 11:1, *"Oros HaYam," Kelim* 17:13.

1. The word Mikvah alone occurs only once in the Bible, ·in Isaiah 22:11. Otherwise, it is usually called a "gathering (*Mikveh*) of water." Cf. Genesis 1:10, Exodus 7:10.
2. *Yerushalmi, Chagigah* 1:8 (7a).
3. *Yoreh Deah* 201:23. See note 9.
4. *Yoreh Deah* 201:6. See *Pesachim* 16b, *Sifra* on Leviticus 11:36 (#143), *Tosefos, Pesachim* 17b *"Eleh," Baba Basra* 66b *"MiKlal,"* HaGra on *Yoreh Deah* 198:29, 201:29.
5. *Yoreh Deah* 201:2, *Sifra* on Leviticus 11:36 (#145), *Yad, Mikvaos* 10:16, Rashi, *Shabbos* 65b *"VeSavar," Tosefos,* ibid. *"Shema,"* Rashi, *Niddah* 67a *"Mikvaos," Tosefos, Bechoros* 55a *"Shema."* Cf. *Mikvaos* 1:7, 5:4, 5, *Tosefos, Chagigah* 11a *"BaMey."*
6. *Yoreh Deah* 201:3, *Sifra* on Leviticus 11:36 (#143). There is a question as to whether the fact that·drawn water renders a Mikvah unfit is a rabbinical law (*DeRabanan*) or a Torah law (*DeOraisa*). The accepted opinion is that if the majority of the water is drawn, then the Mikvah is unfit from Torah law, while if only a minority is drawn, it is unfit by rabbinical law; *Yoreh Deah* 201:3 in *Hagah, Shach* 201:141, *Taz* 201:81. See *Tosefos, Baba Basra* 66b *"MiKlal,"* R. Gershom ibid., R. Yaakov, quoted in *Sefer Mitzvos Gadol (Smag),* positive commandment 248, R. Shimon, quoted in *Shiltey Giborim, Shavuos* (Rif 5a) #1, Rosh, *Baba Kama* 7:3, *Mikva'os* 1 (after *Niddah*), *Tshuvos HaRosh* 31:11, Ritva, *Pesachim* 17b. Also see Rashi, *Baba Kama* 67a, Rashbam, *Baba Basra* 66b *"LeOlam."* Another opinion, however, maintains that the entire rule forbidding drawn water is only rabbinical, see *Yad, Mikvaos* 4:1, 2, R. Yitzchok, quoted in *Tosefos, Pesachim* 17b *"Eleh," Baba Basra,* loc. cit., Ran, *Shavuos* (Rif 5a), Bertenoro on *Mikvaos* 2:3. A third opinion is that of R. Shimshon, who concludes that drawn water is only unfit by Torah law if it also violates rule 6, and is drawn with vessels that can become unclean, R. Shimshon (Rash) on *Mikvaos* 2:3, *Tosefos Yom Tov* ibid., Ran *loc. cit.* A final opinion is that of the Raavad, who maintains that if water is drawn by vessels alone, it is only unfit by rabbinical law, but if drawn by man, then it is unfit by Torah law. Raavad, quoted in *Shitah MeKubetzes, Baba Kama* 67a, Ran, *loc. cit.* For a general discussion, see *Bais Yosef, Yoreh Deah* 201 (p. 97b).
7. *Yoreh Deah* 201:34, *Shach* 201:76, *Taz* 201:43. See *Zevachim* 25b, R. Shimshon, Bertenoro, on *Para* 6:4, *Mikvaos* 5:5; Rosh, *Mikvaos* 5:12, *Tshuvos HaRosh* 31:7. R. Shimshon on *Mikvaos* 2:3 writes that this is a Torah law. Raavad, however, quoted in *Shitah MeKubetzes,* Ran, *loc. cit.,* maintains that this is merely a rabbinical law. There is an opinion that this requirement only applies to "living water" (*Mayim Chayim*), see Mordecai, *Shabuos* 746, Rambam on *Eduyos* 7:4, *Parah* 6:4, *Mikvaos* 5:5, *Yad, Parah Adumah* 6:8, *Mishneh Acharonah* on *Parah loc. cit., Bais Yosef, Yoreh Deah* 201 (p. 109b) *"VeHaRambam," Chidushey R. Chaim HaLevi* on *Yad, Mikvaos* 9:9 (end). Raavad on *Eduyos* 7:4 seems to concur with this opinion, but maintains that in the case of Mikvah, this is a rabbinical law, as men-

tioned earlier. For a complete discussion, see *Tshuvos Chasam Sofer, Yoreh Deah* 199.

8. *Yoreh Deah* 201:1. This is equivalent to three cubic *Amos*, see note 26. According to *Taharos Mayim* 20a, quoted in *Shaarim Metzuyanim KeHalacha* (on *Kitzur Shulchan Aruch*) 37:14 (#2), this is equivalent to 191 gallons. This is based on an *Amah* of 24.5 inches. Estimates of the *Amah*, however, usually vary between 18 and 24 inches. An 18 inch *Amah* yields 61.4 gallons, while a 24 inch *Amah* yields 177 gallons for the capacity of a Mikvah. Except in an emergency, however, the measure of 191 gallons should be abided by. This would mean that the volume of the *Bor* should be at least 25 cubic feet.

9. *Chulin* 84a, *Sifra* on Leviticus 11:36 (#146).

10. *Yerushalmi, Berachos* 9:5 (67b). *Cf.* Rashi, *Baba Basra* 14a "*Ain Miut*," Maharshal *ad loc.*

11. Rashbam, Ramban, Malbim, Hirsch *ad loc.*, Pnai Yehoshua, *Pesachim* 16a "*Chad DeTelushin.*" *Cf. Sifra* on Leviticus 11:34 (#136), Hirsch *ibid.*

12. *Cf. Sifra ad loc.* #143.

13. *Sifra ad loc.* See note 5.

14. *Yoreh Deah* 201:2. See *Shabbos* 65b, *Nedarim* 40a, *Bechoros* 55b, *Niddah* 87a.

15. We see that *Mikveh Mayim* refers to the container as well from Genesis 1:10. See Bachya *ad loc.*, from Isaiah 11:9, where we find that the water "covers the sea."

16. *Zevachim* 25b. See note 7.

17. *Parah* 5:8, *Mikvaos* 6:7, *Yebamos* 15a, *Chagigah* 21b; *Yad, Mikvaos* 8:5, 6, *Yoreh Deah* 201:40, 52.

18. Exodus 29:4, 40:12, Leviticus 8:6, 11:32, 14:8, 9; 15:5, 6, 7, 8, 10, 11, 12, 13, 16, 17, 18, 27; 16:4, 24, 26, 28; 17:15, 22:6, Numbers 19:7, 8, 19; 31:23, Deuteronomy 23:12. In three places, however, we find that "washing" does not refer to Mikvah, see Leviticus 1:9, 1:13, 6:21, but these are specifically excluded, see *Sifra ad loc.*

19. Malbim *ad loc.* #143. *Cf.* Hirsch *ad loc.* See *Sifra* (#145), Rashi, *ad loc.*, Rashi, *Pesachim* 16a "*Yihyeh*," R. Chananel *ibid.*, Rashi, *Chulin* 84a "*Ach Mayin.*"

20. Rashi, *Chagigah* 11a "*BaMayim*," Rashbam, *Pesachim* 109a "*KeDeTanya*," Mizrachi, *Sifsey Chachamim*, on Exodus 24:9. *Cf. Sifra* on Leviticus 14:8. Also see *Tosefos, Chagigah* 11a "*BaMey.*"

21. This cannot refer to water taken from the Mikvah, since as soon as it is removed, it can become unclean. See *Eruvin* 4b, Rashbam, *Pesachim* 109b "*Kal Basaro*," Hirsch on Exodus 29:4, *Yad, Mikvaos* 1:7.

22. *Eruvin* 4b, *Yad, Mikvaos* 1:12. *Cf. Sifra*, Rashi, on Leviticus 15:11.

23. *Yoreh Deah* 201:1, *Sifra* (#122) on Leviticus 11:32, Hirsch *ibid.*, *Sefer Mitzvos Gadol (Smag)* positive commandment 248. *Cf. Sifra* on Leviticus 22:6, Rashi, *Eruvin* 4b "*Kal Basaro.*" If any part of the body is not covered by the water, it remains unclean, and in turn makes the rest of the body unclean, *Reshis Chochmah, Shaar HaAhavah* 11 (92a); *Chesed LeAvraham*, quoted in *Taamey HaMinhagim* B26 (p. 501).

24. *Cf.* Isaiah 1:16. Even the "washing of the feet" in Genesis 18:4 refers to

immersion in a Mikvah, see *Zohar* 1:102b. Likewise, the washing of Joseph's face in Genesis 43:31 refers to the washing away of a mood, see *Targum J.* ad loc. The same is also true of the washing of Pharoah's daughter in Exodus 2:5, see *Sotah* 12b, *Sh'mos Rabbah* 1:23, *Tanchuma, Sh'mos* 7.

25. Indeed, *Targum* on 5:10 and 5:13 renders *Rachatz* (wash) as *Taval* (immerse). See *Torah Temimah* on Leviticus 15:33.

26. *Eruvin* 4b, 14b, *Yoma* 31a, *Chagigah* 11a, *Pesachim* 109a.

27. *Tshuvos Rivash* 292-295, quoted in *Tshuvos Chasam Sofer, Yoreh Deah* 209. See *Mikvaos* 6:3.

28. *Gittin* 58b. *Cf. Yoreh Deah* 109:1.

29. The *Gemorah* thus says that the human body is "elevated" (*Olah*) in 40 *Sa'ah*. The expression *Olah*, however, also refers to nullification (*Bitul*), as we find in *Terumos* 4:7 and other places.

30. Hirsch on Exodus 30:18. *Cf.* Exodus 15:6, Judges 10:8. It is also related to the word *Lachatz* (to crush), see *Targum* on Judges 10:8.

THE MYSTERY OF MIKVAH

1. *Zohar* 1:24a, 3:86b, 3:99b, *Likutey Amarim (Tanya)* 1:4 (8a), *Nefesh HaChaim* 1:6 (note "*VeYadua*"), 2:6, *Anaf Yosef* on *Yoma* 28a (in *Eyin Yaakov* #23). *Cf. Sh'mos Rabbah* 20:18, *Tanchuma, Mishpatim* 3; *Koheles Rabbah* 2:26, 3:16, 5:24, 8:16. Also see Isaiah 3:10, *Zohar* 3:29b, 3:227a (end), 3:224 (end).

2. *Derech HaShem* 1:5:2, *Etz Chaim, Shaar MaN U'MaD* 3 (229a). With relation to Mikvah in particular, see *Reshis Chochmah, Shaar HaAhavah* 11.

3. See Hirsch on Genesis 1:9, *Jeshurun* 7:118, 436, 474. Also see *Moreh Nebuchim* 2:30, Abarbanel, introduction, on Genesis 1:2, *Likutey Halachso (Yoreh Deah) Hechshar Kelim* 4:12.

4. Motion may exist, as in a planetary system or clockwork, but this motion is cyclic and cannot result in change.

5. *Cf.* Rashi, Malbim, *Torah Temimah, ad loc., Shabbos* 55b. In *Berashis Rabbah* 98:4, we see that this·refers to Mikvah in particular.

6. Rashi, Abarbanel (introduction), *ad loc.*, Rashi on Deuteronomy 32:11, *Targum J.*, Rashi, Radak, *Metzudos,* on Jeremiah 23:9. See *Chagigah* 15a; *Etz Chayim, Shaar RaPaCh Nitzutzin* 1 (255a).

7. *Yerushalmi, Chagigah* 2:1 (8b), *Mechilta* to Exodus 15:11, *Berashis Rabbah* 4:1, 5:2, *Sh'mos Rabbah* 15:22, *Midrash Tehillim* 104:7, from Psalm 104:3. *Cf.* Job 28:20.

8. *Yad, Yesodey HaTorah* 1:11, *Moreh Nebuchim* 1:11.

9. Ramban,*Likutey Torah* (HaAri), *Shaar HaPesukim, ad loc., Berashis Rabbah* 2:5, *Bahir* 2, *Zohar* 1:16a, 3:305b, *Etz Chaim, loc. cit., Likutey Halachos (Yoreh Deah) Hechsher Kelim* 4:38.

10. *Ibid.* See *Tanchuma, VaYeshev* 4.

11. See Maharzav on *Berashis Rabbah* 2:4, "*Bris Kerusah.*" With regard to how this is related to Mikvah, see *Sefer HaChinuch* 173, *Likutey Halachos, loc. cit.* 4:12, 4:38.

12. *Berashis Rabbah* 2:4, *Zohar* 1:192b. *Cf. Tosefos, Avodah Zarah* 5a *"Ki Ruach."*

13. *Yerushalmi, Berachos* 9:2 (65b), *Taanis* 1:3 (4b); from Psalm 42:8; *Berashis Rabbah* 13:13, *Pirkey DeRabbi Eliezer* 23 (43a), *Etz Chaim, Shaar MaN U'MaD* 1 (p. 221). See note 28.

14. *Cf.* Isaiah 48:1, *Targum, Radak, ad loc.* Also see *Zohar* 1:30a, from Job 38:20.

15. Hirsch on Genesis 1:9, Radal on *Berashis Rabbah* 5:10 #7. *Cf. Moreh Nebuchim* 2:30.

16. Thus, the final formation of plant life actually took place on the sixth day, see *Chulin* 60b, *Berashis Rabbah* 13:1, Rashi, Ramban, on Genesis 2:5; *Zohar* 1:46b, 1:97a, 2:128a. *Cf. Sifra* on Leviticus 26:4.

17. *Yerushalmi Shabbos* 2:6 (20a), *Berashis Rabbah* 14:1, *Sh'mos Rabbah* 30:13. Man was created from male and female elements, see *Berashis Rabbah* 14:7. Also see Rashi on Genesis 6:7.

18. *Yerushalmi, Peah* 1:1 (5a), *Sanhedrin* 10:1 (49a).

19. *Baba Kama* 17a, Rashi on Isaiah 41:17. See *Zohar* 1:25a, that water is the Torah, and its vessel is Israel. Also see Ezekiel 43:2, Amos 8:11, Proverbs 17:14, Job 14:19. For how this relates to Mikvah, see *Berachos* 16a, *Tanna DeBei Eliahu Rabba* 18 (90a), Alshich on Leviticus 14:8, *Nefesh HaChaim* 1:21, *Likutey Halachos (Yoreh Deah) Mikvaos* 1:2, 4:24.

20. Genesis 7:4, 12, 17, 8:6.

21. Exodus 23:18, 24:28, Deuteronomy 9:9, 11, 18, 25, 10:10. We also find that the Tablets weighed forty *Sa'ah, Yerushalmi Taanis* 4:5 (23a), *Tanchuma, Ki Tisa* 26.

22. Exodus 16:35, Deuteronomy 2:7, 8:2, 4, 29:4, Joshua 5:6.

23. Thus, Isaac was forty years old when he married Rebecca (Genesis 25:20), Esau was forty when he married (Genesis 26:34), Jacob was embalmed for forty days (Genesis 50:3), the land was quiet for forty years in the time of the Judges (Judges 3:11, 5:31, 8:28), Elijah fasted for forty days (1 Kings 19:8, *Tanchuma, Sh'mos* 14), during the Babylonian exile, the land was desolate for forty years (Ezekiel 4:6, 29:11, 12). For other important cases, see *Zohar* 1:136b.

24. *Niddah* 31b.

25. *Kerisus* 10a, *Niddah* 30a.

26. *Niddah* 3:7 (30a), 15b; *Mishneh LaMelech* on *Yad, Tumas Mes* 2:1, *Shach, Choshen Mishpat* 210:1, *Tshuvas Toras Chesed, Even HaEzer* 42:33, *Tshuvos Bais Shlomo, Choshen Mishpat* 132. Also see *Ohalos* 18:7, Bertenoro, R. Shimshon, *ad loc.*, Rashi, *Pesachim* 9a *"Arbayim Yom."* The Talmud also euphemistically speaks of conception as being "forty days before the formation of the foetus," *Berachos* 60a, *Sotah* 2a.

27. *Berashis Rabbah* 32:5, Rashi on Genesis 7:4. *Cf. VaYikra Rabbah* 23:12.

28. *Zohar* 1:61b.

29. *Bereshis Rabbah* 32:5, *Likutey Halachos (Yoreh Deah) Nedarim* 2:11. See *Zohar* 1:136b.

30. *Pardes Rimonim* 16:1, 19:2, *Shaarey Kedushah* 3:6, *Derech HaSheim* 4:6:13. These are the four universes, *Atzilus* (Emination), *Beriah* (creation), *Yetzira* (formation) and *Asiyah* (making or action).

89

31. *Derech HaShem, ibid.* This is the world of *Sefiros* (Eminations).
32. Radak on Isaiah 43:7, *Nefesh HaChaim* 1:13 (note *"U'Lefi"*).
33. *Avos* 5:1.
34. These are Genesis 1:3, 1:6, 1:9, 1:11, 1:14, 1:20, 1:24, 1:26, 1:28, and 1:29.
35. *Reshis Chochmah, Shaar HaAhavah* 11, *Shnei Luchos HaBris, Shaar HaOsios, Taharah* (1:108a). In Kabbalah, this refers to the four *Yud's* in the Name adding up to 72 (*Ab*). See sources quoted in part 1, note 20. This is closely related to the fact that Adam, Eve, the Serpent, and the earth, each received ten punishments, making a total of forty. See *Pirkey DeRabbi Eliezer* 14, *BaMidbar Rabbah* 5:5, *Tanchuma, BaMidbar* 23, *Zohar* 3:280b.
36. *Shabbos* 7:2 (73a).
37. *Cf.* HaGra *ad loc.* The forty categories of work parallel the forty times that the word *Malachah* (work) appears in the Torah, *Shabbos* 49b, *Yerushalmi Shabbos* 7:2 (42a). One of these forty, however, is not counted.
38. *Tikuney Zohar* 19 (39a), according to reading of *Kisey Melech,* HaGra *ad loc., Adir BaMarom* 89b, *Reshis Chochmah, Shaar HaAhavah* 11 (92a), *Shnei Luchos HaBris, Shaar HaOsios, Kedushah* 1:168a. For the relationship of *Mem* to water, see *Sefer Yetzira* 3:4, *Zohar* 2:159b, *Likutey Moharan* 51, *Likutey Halachos (Yoreh Deah) Gerim* 3:4. Gramatically, the Hebrew word *Mayim* is literally the plural of the plain letter *Mem*.
39. *Sefer Yetzira* 3:4, *Bahir* 85, *Etz Chaim, Shaar HaYereach* 3 (p. 176).
40. *Bahir* 84.
41. *Berashis Rabbah* 81:2. *Cf. Shabbos* 55a.
42. *Avos* 2:9, *Tamid* 32a. See *Adir BaMarom* 37b.
43. Note that the word *Sa'ah* is phonetically related to *Sha'ah,* meaning "hour." Actually, it is the surface of the Mikvah that is involved in the purification, and this surface represents the interface between past and future. This surface is represented by the Name *Ekyeh,* which literally means "I will become." See *Keser Shem Tov* 2, and other references in part 1, notes 18 and 20.
44. *Moreh Nebuchim* 1:2, 2:6, *Kuzari* 4:1 (2b), Ibn Ezra on Genesis 1:1, Exodus 3:15, 33:21, Ramban on Exodus 3:13.
45. *Orech Chaim* 5:1, *Cf. Likutey Amarim (Tanya)* 2:6 (80a), *Nefesh HaChaim* 1:2.
46. *Mechilta* on Exodus 15:2, *Sifra* on Leviticus 18:2; *Berashis Rabbah* 33:3, 73:3, *Midrash Tehillim* 47:2, *Pesikta* 22 (151b), Rashi on Genesis 1:1, Hoseah 14:2, *Rokeach* 200.
47. *Likutey Amarim (Tanya)* 2:4 (79a), *Nefesh HaChaim* 2:2 (end). *Cf. Moreh Nebuchim* 1:61.
48. *Orech Chaim* 5:1, HaGra *ad loc., Shnei Luchos HaBris, Bais HaShem* 1:40b, *Mesechta Shavuos* 2:100a.
49. *Rosh HaShanah* 18a. *Cf.* Rambam, *Tosefos Yom Tov, Rosh HaShanah* 1:2.
50. See note 46. Also see *Taz, Orech Chaim* 621:2, *Prim Megadim ad loc.*
51. *Ikkarim* 4:27. *Cf. Nesivos Olam, Tshuvah* 5.
52. *Sanhedrin* 8:7 (73a).
53. *Yoma* 86b. *Cf. Etz Yosef* (in *Eyin Yaakov* # 76) *ad loc.*
54. See Rashi on Exodus 34:6, *Rosh HaShanah* 17b, that the doubling of God's

name in this verse, *"HaShem, HaShem,"* means that God is the same before and after the sin. The idea that the Name *HaShem* relates to mercy is derived from this verse, see *Berashis Rabbah* 33:3, 73:3.

55. *Likutey Halachos (Yoreh Deah) Milah* 4:23. See Ezekiel 36:29, *Yalkut* 2:627, *Tikuney Zohar* 19 (39a), *Keser Shem Tov* 2, *Baal Shem Tov, Yisro* 11. The water of the Mikvah therefore alludes to the letters in God's Name, see references in part 1, note 20.
56. See Hirsch on Genesis 1:9.
57. Hirsch on Leviticus 5:13, 7:20, 11:43.
58. *Targum ad loc.*, Rashi, *Niddah* 9a *"Lo Echad,"* *Likutey Moharan* 51. Cf. *Zohar* 1:12a, Ezekiel 37:23.

Typical structure of a modern Mikvah